Emotional SMARTS!®

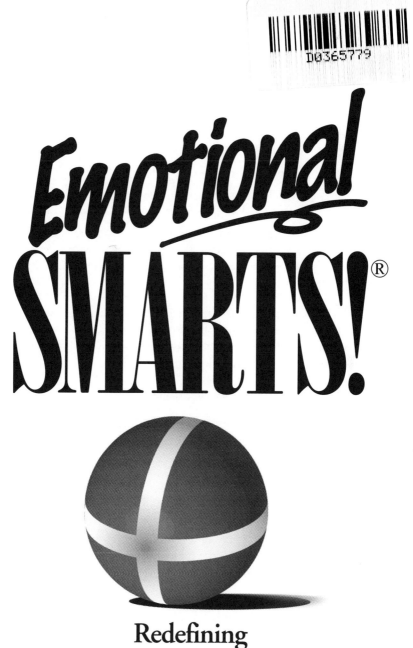

Redefining
Personal & Professional Competence

June Donaldson, MBA, EdD
Certified Mediator and Arbitrator

Emotional SMARTS!®
by
June Donaldson, MBA, EdD, Certified Mediator and Arbitrator

Sixth Printing, Revised Edition – September, 2005

Copyright © 1997, 1998, 2002, 2003, 2004, 2005 by Donaldson & Associates, Inc.

The Emotional SMARTS!® book and Emotional SMARTS!® Self-Scoring Profile are based on theoretical concepts, organizational and practical experience. They are not a scientific measure of emotional intelligence and are not intended for diagnostic or selection purposes. They are tools which provide information on emotional intelligence concepts and professional development. The Emotional SMARTS!® Self-Scoring Profile has no relationship to the products of Multi-Health Systems Inc. including the BarOn Emotional Intelligence Quotient Inventory (EQ-i®). Individuals or organizations wishing to obtain emotional intelligence materials for diagnostic or selection purposes are directed to registered psychologists.

For more information, please contact:
Dr. June Donaldson
Donaldson & Associates Inc., 499 – 1919B – 4th Street, S.W.
Calgary, Alberta, Canada T2S 1W4, Telephone: (403) 287-2244
Fax: (403) 287-1212, Website: www.emotionalsmarts.com

Canadian Cataloguing in Publication Data

Donaldson, June, 1944-

Emotional smarts!® : redefining personal & professional competence / June Donaldson. – Rev. ed. –

emotional intelligence and emotional quotient

ISBN 1-894022-88-2

1. Success in business.   I. Title.
HF5386.D65 2003   650.1   C2003-910009-X

Cover Design by Brian Danchuk, Regina, Saskatchewan

Designed, Printed and Produced in Canada by:
Centax Books, a Division of PrintWest Communications Ltd.
Publishing Director – Margo Embury
1150 Eighth Avenue, Regina, Saskatchewan, Canada S4R 1C9
(306) 525-2304   Fax: (306) 757-2439
E-mail: centax@printwest.com   www.centaxbooks.com

Critical Reviews of Emotional SMARTS!®

"This book provides us with practical reinforcement of core values in a vastly changing environment. June is to be commended with her direct approach and an easy-reading book."

Al Coates, Senior Vice-President, Business Operations
Anaheim Mighty Ducks, Anaheim, California, U.S.A.

"June's book, *Emotional SMARTS!*® is a truly refreshing approach to an ever-escalating problem of coping with impossible demands upon our time and attention. More importantly, this book provides the reader with insightful techniques on how to analyze ourselves and those we interact with, to improve our overall quality of life versus the traditional 'business only' focus. I found this book personally helpful in assisting me to regroup and energize."

Rick Derouin, Senior Director Business Development
Server Technologies, Oracle Corporation, Toronto, Ontario, Canada

"Extraordinary – compelling – an extremely useful presentation of *Emotional SMARTS!*® which will make every day another glorious day in which to excel – life is indeed good!"

Wallace N. Hall, Manager NGL Operations
Dome Pipeline Corporation, Iowa City, IA, U.S.A.

"This book simplifies emotional intelligence concepts to where people, especially those involved in management, marketing, sales and customer service, have a workable process to use in demonstrating their Emotional *SMARTS!*® with clients, colleagues, peers, family and friends. Considering the pace, intensity, and demands of business, Dr. Donaldson's work is timely, appropriate, and important to organizational success."

Bryant Jackson, President and CEO
Metafore Corporation, Calgary, Alberta, Canada

"High-performing business professionals need more than financial understanding and strategic acumen to succeed; they need Emotional SMARTS!® Dr. Donaldson's very accessible, easily-remembered framework will help our associates leverage emotional intelligence not only to improve relationships, but to get bottom-line results."

Ron Lawrence, Director, Leadership & Executive Development
Capital One Services, Inc., Richmond, Virginia, U.S.A.

Critical Reviews of Emotional SMARTS!®

"*Emotional SMARTS!® Redefining Personal and Professional Competence* is a down-to-earth guide for making our world a better place. Dr. Donaldson presents practical principles of self-management and relationship building not usually found between the covers of one book. This is a must-read for anyone who wants to be happy and successful at and away from work."
> Colleen Lemire, M.Ed.,
> Manager, Employee Development and Communications
> Jacobs Canada Inc., Calgary, Alberta, Canada

"June should be commended for providing this concise and readable book dealing with emotional strength and well-being. This book will appeal to a large segment of the population who will benefit from the practicality of the timely advice offered."
> Ann McCaig, Past Chancellor
> University of Calgary, Calgary, Alberta, Canada

"In today's demanding and intense times, one's ability to be emotionally smart is at the foundation of them being able to manage change, lead, work in teams, negotiate and handle conflict. Dr. June's easy to understand, relate to, and apply emotional intelligence model and process should be at the foundation of organizational learning, leadership and development programs."
> Norm Trainor, President and CEO,
> The Covenant Group, Toronto, Ontario, Canada

"In these days of on-going change and uncertainty, being emotionally intelligent is a critical business and relationship skill. Dr. Donaldson's book simplifies this important concept and should make the language and behaviors of Emotional SMARTS!® commonplace in relationships and organizations."
> Nick Valvano, Chief Executive Officer
> V Foundation for Cancer Research, Raleigh, North Carolina, U.S.A.

Dedication

This guidebook is dedicated to all the

sad, bad, mad, and scary

people, places, and times

I have known,

because without them

my work on this subject

and my survival through the "tough times"

would never have happened.

The Author

June Donaldson, MBA, EdD, Certified Mediator and Arbitrator, is a business consultant, best-selling author, newspaper columnist, keynote speaker, conference, and seminar facilitator. June integrates her emotional intelligence work, known as Emotional SMARTS!®, with how people manage with change, lead, work in teams, provide customer service and sales, negotiate, and manage conflict.

Dr. Donaldson's experience in corporate and branch-office management, marketing, sales, administration, training, and professional development; her work in the public sector; and her experience as an entrepreneur ideally position her to link emotional intelligence competencies and skills, as outlined in the Emotional SMARTS!® model, with workplace and home life performance and related results.

June has a Diploma in Adult Education from St. Francis Xavier University; a Master of Business Administration (MBA) degree from Gonzaga University in Spokane, Washington; a Doctor of Education degree, with a specialization in Adult Learning; and accreditation as a certified Mediator and Arbitrator with the Alberta (Canada) Arbitration and Mediation Society.

Donaldson & Associates Inc. is located in Calgary, Alberta, Canada. The company provides keynote and conference presentations, business consulting, management retreat and seminar facilitation on a broad range of topics to its domestic and international client base. In addition, services are provided in Alternative Dispute Resolution (ADR) activities such as mediation, arbitration, med-arb, and conflict management system design. Services have been provided throughout Canada, the United States, Asia Pacific, and the Caribbean.

Table of Contents

A heartfelt thank you to ...

Jean Hendry who, in 1991, posed a life-changing question:
"Have you ever heard of Gonzaga University?"

Father Bernard J. Coughlin S.J., Father Tony Lehmann S.J.,
Dean Clarence Barnes, Terry Coombes,
and the faculty and staff of
The School of Business, Gonzaga University
in Spokane, Washington
who gave me the learning opportunity of a lifetime.

Clive Pringle and the staff of Gateway Data Solutions Inc,
Calgary, Alberta
who kept the home office fires burning
for my return to Canada.

Margo Embury, Dan Marce, Iona Glabus, and the staff of
PrintWest Communications for their competence,
dedication, and skill in making this book come to life.

My special family, wonderful friends, and supportive clients who
kept the faith, and demonstrated their support with words and
deeds of encouragement along the path of building
Emotional SMARTS!®

The Logo

The logo represents the universe and how people think and feel about their emotions. Some people are inclusive in their thinking and feeling, and that is represented by the circle. Others are more structured in their approach, and that is represented by the bars within the circle.

The four quadrants represent the A, B, C, D of demonstrating Emotional SMARTS!® On the cover, the blue tones on the left side of the logo indicate cool, clear thinking, while the red tones on the right side of the logo represent the emotional side of who we are. This could be interpreted as our intellectual intelligence, our IQ, blending with our emotional intelligence, or EQ.

Lastly, the logo represents a ball which is moving and dynamic, similar to how our emotions react to our life experiences. Perhaps the best part of the logo is that a ball is always balanced, just as we can be when we demonstrate our Emotional SMARTS!®

Special Credits
Editing: M. Louise Gallagher, Calgary, Alberta
Initial Logo Design: Doug Martin, Calgary, Alberta
Illustrations: Diane Kathrens, Calgary, Alberta

Emotional SMARTS!® — An Overview

On your path to Emotional SMARTS!® know that . . .

1. You will not have to disclose your life secrets in this guidebook!

2. You will not have to learn how to give or receive air kisses!

3. You will not have to hug anyone (unless you both think it's a good idea)!

As you explore your Emotional SMARTS!® know that . . .

Emotional SMARTS!® is about far more than just affairs of the heart. It's about taking responsibility for how you live and manage your life and relationships.

Emotional SMARTS!® is a powerful new emotional intelligence framework for people who want to understand how to maximize their psychological wellness, relationships, decision making, and results.

Emotional SMARTS!® can be improved upon unlike intellectual intelligence (IQ) which is said to be static.

Emotional SMARTS!® "de-acamademicacizes" or demystifies emotional intelligence concepts and identifies the A, B, C, Ds, of being emotionally smart. Emotional SMARTS!® specifically focuses on:

- **Awareness Skills**

- **Behavioral Skills**

- **Contact Skills**

- **Decision-Making Skills**

Emotional SMARTS!® is our willingness and ability to identify and manage our emotional wellness, particularly during times of ongoing change, challenge and conflict in our relationships, home life, workplace, health, wellness, and aging. Demonstrating our Emotional SMARTS!® results in integrating our intellectual intelligence (IQ); our ability to comprehend, reason and measure, with our emotional intelligence (EQ) so we are able to fluently self-manage, appropriately behave in a wide variety of settings, contact or connect well with diverse people, and make decisions that stand the test of time and scrutiny.

Most people don't give their Emotional SMARTS!® a second thought when life is nice and normal, and people are pleasant and predictable. However, when life goes "sideways" on us; when we are faced with work challenges, relationship issues, child or elder-care concerns, health anxieties, or financial worries, our ability to stay emotionally smart can be seriously tested. It is during these times that we need to demonstrate our Emotional SMARTS!® by being grounded, centered, and focused. Only then will we achieve the best results possible for our investment of time, money, energy, resources, and talent.

Unfortunately, today many people are fearful, frustrated, and fatigued – made so by the fragile nature and unrelenting change in organizations, family structures, and our world communities. People are fearful because they don't know what the future holds for them in terms of safety, security, recognition, opportunity; they are frustrated because they have lost their "voice" or perceived sphere of involvement and influence; they are fatigued by unrelenting change and increased responsibilities in their relationships, families, work, and communities. Our collective psyche is stretched. Now more than ever, each of us must work at building, protecting, and demonstrating our Emotional SMARTS!® on a daily basis.

In short, people with Emotional SMARTS!® take charge of their emotional wellness and related successes. They take ownership for managing themselves, their behaviors, their relationships, and their life decisions. They do this in both their personal and professional lives.

From a business perspective, corporate dysfunction, inadequate management skills, and employee resistance to change are identified as the top three barriers to corporate restructuring success. However, before we come down too hard on the "system", remember – we are the system. Let's make sure we operate with Emotional SMARTS!® in our professional lives as we contribute to the production, performance, and prosperity of our organization. Ultimately, if we don't demonstrate Emotional SMARTS!® in our business activities, in time, we won't have an organization to worry about because the organization will cease to exist.

The time has come for all business people – from the executive team to the front lines – to understand and endorse the cornerstones and characteristics of Emotional SMARTS!® Why? Because people with Emotional SMARTS!® are the ones who breathe spirit, direction, and results into the strategic plans and operational processes of organizations. When that happens, organizations have a better chance of meeting their goals – fiscally, procedurally, and operationally.

This book, while not written to be a scholarly or academic masterpiece, is designed to be an educational, encouraging, affordable, easy-to-read, book about how to identify, build, and maintain your emotional intelligence. The Emotional SMARTS!® model was created as a result of scholarly work and literature reviews surveyed as I completed my doctoral studies; a wide variety of life experiences; a significant background in management, marketing, major account sales, plus the design and facilitation of non-technical, management, sales, interpersonal, and communication-skills programs.

As you read the book, you will recognize many of the topics. For example, it probably won't be the first time you are reminded of the importance of assertiveness, stress management, or creative problem solving. It might, though, be the first time you are provided with a framework of four critical cornerstones and sixteen specific characteristics that are interdependent, and require consistent performance if you want to be in an overall state of emotional wellness.

Challenge yourself to examine how each of the cornerstones and characteristics are present in your life. I have provided examples of things you might do when you are emotionally unaware or emotionally smart, but you are the resident expert on the state of your Emotional SMARTS!® So, as you reflect on the general examples given, ask yourself what specifically you might need to do to improve your results within each of the characteristics.

When you finish reading this book, my hope is that you will be motivated to identify Emotional SMARTS!® characteristics you might improve upon, and then take specific action to enhance skills that will enable you to increase your results and "shine" even more than you already do.

Good luck in your journey!

Sincerely,

June Donaldson

Emotional SMARTS!® Framework

The following framework represents the four major corner-stones of Emotional SMARTS!® and the characteristics associated with each. The four cornerstones: **Awareness Skills, Behavioral Skills, Contact Skills, and Decision-Making Skills** are interdependent and can all be improved upon, independently or in concert with another.

AWARENESS SKILLS

Emotional Self-Awareness
Emotional Management
Assertiveness
Goal Achievement
Optimism

BEHAVIORAL SKILLS

Self-Reliance
Stress Management
Impulse Control
Conflict Management

CONTACT SKILLS

Relationship Building
Empathy
Community Care

DECISION-MAKING SKILLS

Problem Identification
Creativity
Selecting Solutions
Reality Testing

C H A P T E R   1

AWARENESS SKILLS

Awareness skills relate to our ability to consistently identify and manage our emotions as we deal with life's issues. We are able to manage our emotions in an assertive and optimistic manner as we stay focused on achieving what is important to us. The five characteristics of the Awareness cornerstone are:

Emotional Self-Awareness

Emotional Management

Assertiveness

Goal Achievement

Optimism

Awareness Skills

Emotional Self-Awareness

Emotional self-awareness forms the foundation of Emotional SMARTS!® When we are emotionally self-aware, we are able to recognize, identify, and appropriately acknowledge our feelings in all that we do, personally and professionally.

This characteristic is tough for many business people because our business environments reward us for thinking and doing – not feeling. As a result, many of us have been conditioned to think of our feelings in terms of:

> I'm okay. OR I'm not okay.
>
> I'm fine. OR I'm not fine.
>
> I'm stressed. OR I'm not stressed.

None of which say enough.

These statements don't tell the individual or others what's going on internally with the speaker. Trust of ourselves or with others is nearly impossible to build if we are not prepared to identify and discuss how we feel about people, places, and things. Appropriate disclosure – characterized by openness – is one of the consistent themes in building and maintaining trusting relationships.

I am not saying we need to overwhelm ourselves and others with emotional self-indulgence. What I am saying is the greatest single gift we can give ourselves in the area of emotional intelligence is to identify how we feel about events that take place around us, or to us. We must work at building our emotional vocabulary and being emotionally literate on a consistent basis. If we don't understand the circumstances and state our feelings about situations in a timely and appropriate way, we run the risk of being perceived as emotionally bankrupt, as non-assertive, as a pushover or, in the other extreme, as an aggressive corporate bully or psychopath in a suit. In time, we may shut down emotionally to the point where we can't even find the feelings, never mind feel the feelings, identify the feelings, process the feelings, and resiliently recover from the feelings.

So, the next time you are driving home, talking to your steering wheel about something that happened to you, or around you, six weeks ago, or you are telling your story to a stranger who is sitting beside you on the transit system, instead of trying to make sense of it in your head, let your heart do the talking. Start by identifying how you feel about the situation and why you might feel that way?

For example, do you know there are a minimum of eight feeling categories? When we experience work and life events, our feelings can range in intensity through eight major categories:

mad	surprised
sad	shamed
glad	disgusted
scared	loved

Feeling words are interrelated and we can experience more than one category at a time. The following list, while extensive, does not include every possible feeling word, so add those that are important to you.

MAD

antagonistic	indignant	obnoxious	exasperated	fuming
unhappy	resentment	bitter	furious	hostile
angry	annoyance	rage	wrath	loathing
provoked	animosity	mean	hatred	destructive
combative	spiteful	outraged	deceitful	cruel
impatient	sullen	violent	vengeful	ticked off

Other: _____ _____ _____ _____

SAD

abandoned	restless	hopeless	undervalued	grief
bad	sorrow	apathetic	unwanted	gloom
discontent	melancholy	gloomy	despair	belittled
disturbed	lonely	miserable	dejected	diminished
lethargic	unhappy	helpless	depressed	divided
unpopular	emotional	terrible	self-pity	exhausted
hurt	tired	homesick	weak	torn-up
indifferent	unimportant	uncared for	dismayed	cheated
upset	dissatisfied	pained	degraded	listless
weepy	ugly	defeated	crushed	dismal
low	lost	fatigued	empty	defeated
ignored	unsatisfied	weary	rejected	fed-up
solemn	forlorn	sick	resigned	left-out
worn-out	horrible	unloved	apprehensive	overwhelmed

Other: _____ _____   _____ _____

GLAD

content	pleased	excited	thrilled	worthy
cheerful	playful	calm	rapture	respected
happy	spontaneous	clever	delighted	adequate
joyous	eager	important	ecstasy	beautiful
amused	venturous	joyful	euphoric	capable
warm	attuned	childish	peaceful	vibrant
liked	esteemed	silly	courageous	independent
jolly	good	relieved	great	proud
graced	inspired	nice	gratified	worthy
patient	appreciated	keen	elated	brave
valued	admired	pleasant	helpful	satisfied
enlightened	optimistic	high	brilliant	rewarded
relaxed	free	wonderful	helpful	satisfied
overjoyed	gratified	tickled	safe	trusting

Other: _____ _____   _____ _____

SCARED

anxious	distracted	dubious	frightened	petrified
nervous	disturbed	estingy	panic	afraid
concerned	unsure	frantic	phobic	distraught
misgivings	reluctant	hysterical	terrified	moody
wary	mixed-up	tentative	fearful	worried
edgy	suspicious	apprehensive	dread	tense
consternation	confused	uneasy	intimidated	dreadful
stressed	troubled	unsettled	vulnerable	threatened
shaken	alarmed	trapped	burdened	uncomfortable

Other: _____ _____ _____ _____

SURPRISED

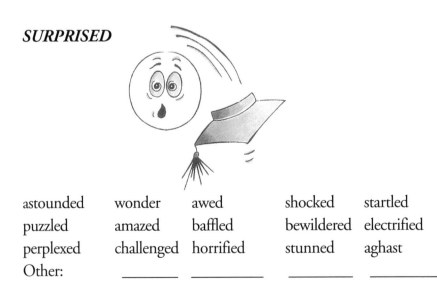

astounded	wonder	awed	shocked	startled
puzzled	amazed	baffled	bewildered	electrified
perplexed	challenged	horrified	stunned	aghast

Other: _____ _____ _____ _____

SHAMED

wicked	embarrassed	stupid	guilty	conned
odd	chagrined	empty	remorse	useless
dependent	regretful	alone	humiliation	unloved
timid	insecure	unwanted	unlovable	mortified
screwed up	sneaky	unsupported	worthless	divided
isolated	inadequate	unworthy	strange	impotent
futile	estranged	conspicuous	persecuted	disdain

Other: _____ _____ _____ _____

DISGUSTED

skeptical	aversion	condemning	abhorrence	revulsion
pity	distaste	obsessed	scorn	contempt
repugnant	nauseated	loath	offended	sickened

Other: _____ _____ _____ _____

LOVED

safe	acceptance	calm	adoration	enchanted
fascinated	friendship	immortal	infatuated	blissful
joyous	kindly	obsessed	trusting	loved
inspired	affinity	handsome	amorous	tender
honored	special	renewed	idolized	passionate
affectionate	at ease	rapture	desirable	heavenly
loving	charmed	lustful	sexy	connected
captivated	pretty	intrigued	unique	light-hearted

Other: _____   _____   _____   _____

Whether we like it or not, if a situation is troubling us we need to deal with it in a timely and appropriate way. If we are demonstrating our Emotional SMARTS!® we will identify:

1. The actual event that has triggered emotion.

2. How we are feeling (not thinking!) about the event?

3. Why we feel the way we feel?

4. Previous emotionally charged events that might be connected to, or similar to, the current situation?

5. How to best manage our feelings so that negative or sad emotions don't overwhelm us and result in our saying or doing something that could become a CLM (Career Limiting Move)?

Emotionally Unaware reactions could be:

- To not disclose your feelings to a person directly involved in the emotionally charged situation because you assume disclosure will make you a weakling. When you talk about how you feel about situations, you establish boundaries in relationships. Boundaries help create respectful relationships because the other person learns your limits and expectations and you learn theirs!

- To assume you can "keep the peace" by not saying how you feel. If anything, not talking about your feelings, going underground, will foster more toxicity as time goes on. In time it could result in you acting out in a way that damages your reputation, credibility, sphere of influence, and results.

- To believe a difficult situation will go away if you just leave it alone and don't do or say anything. (It has been my experience that the longer I leave difficult situations, the faster they expand to 147 times their original size.)

- To believe the other person SHOULD know how you feel without your telling them.

Responses that use your Emotional SMARTS!® are:

- To become skilled at identifying how you are feeling at any time of the day or night over any issue that comes up. You don't have to tell anyone what you are doing, but on a regular basis and in your head, ask yourself:

  > What's going on with me right now? How am I feeling about ____?

  > Am I mad, sad, glad, scared, surprised, shamed, disgusted, loved, or all of the above?

  > Why am I feeling this way?

- To become skilled at discussing your feelings, in a clear, concise and nondefensive way, with others who have a right or a need to know.

For example, learn to process your thoughts and feelings using the following formula:

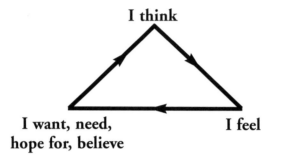

When you are able to formulate and share your thoughts, feelings, and needs in this manner, you help yourself become clear on what is important to you. As well, you help others understand where you are coming from and what you need to function well in the relationship. An added bonus is that you will find out what others need or want from the relationship. When you present things in this way, you can de-emotionalize emotional topics because you have a path to follow in preparing for your discussion. It will also help you be clean and clear about how you communicate.

- Taking courses on assertiveness, self-esteem, communication skills, interpersonal skills – there are plenty to choose from. Check your local university or college, continuing education programs, the YWCA or YMCA for life-long learning options. If you live in a rural area or your schedule doesn't permit taking a structured daytime course, check out the many distance-learning opportunities that are being introduced to the marketplace.

- Reading – the bookshelves are overflowing with books about emotional intelligence and psychological soundness.

- Looking into participating in a mentoring, support, or counselling group. These types of groups can be educational and
often lessen the isolation one feels when dealing with changing
environments. Often, these groups can help you validate and
build your knowledge and skills. They can assist you to confirm
whether you are building and protecting your psychological well
being in the most appropriate way.

I have never understood reluctance to utilize the benefits of a
support group environment. Think of this! We are born. We have
no training on how to live and we rely on our parents to be our
teachers. Sometimes they know how to parent, or they know a little about parenting, or they know nothing about parenting. In
some cases, we grow up with limited education, role models, and
guidelines on how to live with our Emotional SMARTS!® fully acti-
vated. So, having a learning venue like a support or mentoring
program, or even an Employee Assistance Program, can be a
method of checking to see if we are on the right track.

Remember, what we learn from 0 to 7, we take with us from 8
to 80. Are we taking the right material with us? Is the material we
base our decisions on appropriate and realistic for us in our current
environment? OR, do we need to develop the courage to house-
clean, getting rid of old attitudes, unrewarding environments,
unhealthy behaviors, and toxic relationships.

Awareness Skills

Emotional Management

Emotional management is our ability to monitor our feelings and behaviors so our actions are appropriate to the situation. It is our ability to soothe, encourage, or motivate ourselves during difficult times.

When we are skilled at managing our emotions, we don't become too high when things are going well or too low when things are discouraging. We are able to keep ourselves grounded and centered so that we feel a sense of control over our feelings, behavior, and the outcomes in our lives.

This is not always easy.

Let's say something happened at work that overwhelmed and demoralized you. Since it happened, you have had difficulty getting fired up for your work, the company, or even some of the people you work with. So, what's the answer? How are you going to manage your emotions so you do not say or do something that is Emotionally Unaware?

A starting point might be to ask yourself whether the situation is any of your business. It's true, many times we get emotionally choked up about things that are really none of our business. We need to ensure we are managing our emotions on the right topic, with the right people, in the right way, and for the right reasons.

Now, let's say you determine the situation is some of your business, e.g., you are going to be directly affected by what is happening.

Some Emotionally Unaware things to do could be to:

- Tell someone "off" and not create an opportunity to talk and listen with the other person.

- Swear, name call, or say things that are reputation destroying or threatening. Don't think this doesn't happen. ***For example***, a businessman has travelled extensively, he arrives back at the office and discovers he can't find an important file. Feeling panicked, tired, and scared, he accuses his administrative assistant of doing something with the file. The administrative assistant has never seen the file, and yet fields verbal abuse about her incompetence at running the office. In time, the file is found in the side pocket of the boss's laptop computer case. The individual never acknowledges or apologizes for his behavior, damaging or hurtful comments.

- Quit your job, without having another job, and then, for good measure, write a "hate" letter and send it to the company president.

- Pilfer time (excessive personal time and long lunches), resources (time and effort on second-rate work), supplies (pencils, paper, calculators, computers, or company vehicles), and/or money (hard cash or soft dollars) from the organization because, "They owe me."

- Develop an "I'll show them" attitude. It may feel good at the time but it is only a matter of time until the company shows you by managing you out of the business.

- Send angry and demeaning e-mail messages to a cast of thousands in the company because you are frustrated.

- Live from a base of career fear where you spend your time, effort, and resources planning, positioning, and protecting yourself at the expense of your family, friends, work, team, and organization. (Remember, it's tough to get your shoulder into the load if you're constantly watching your back.)

Approaches that incorporate your Emotional SMARTS!® could be to:

- Memorize images, statements, or encouraging thoughts to help you stabilize your emotions and keep the situation you are experiencing in perspective. My mother used to say that when you were feeling low or hard done by, it was important to "take a bus ride". There will always be someone on that bus who appears sadder, more alone, more frustrated, or more disadvantaged than you.

- Get real about how you feel! Often when we experience difficulties, we intellectualize the situation, trying to rationalize who did what to whom and why they did it. This approach denies the intensity of what we are feeling by moving us to a place of evaluating, assessing, judging, and thereby distancing ourselves from the situation on an emotional basis. The next time you are tempted to intellectualize an emotional event, challenge yourself to identify how you are feeling (not what you are thinking), and continue to ask yourself, "Am I mad, sad, glad, scared, feeling surprise, shame, disgust, or love?" Don't let yourself off the hook because there might be some pain in thinking about the emotional side of the situation. You will know when you have identified authentic emotions about the situation because your body, if you are listening, will send you signals of relief.

- Train yourself to consistently evaluate why you feel the way you do when certain things happen to you. Turn the rocks over. Develop a critical eye and an inquisitive heart so you can assess situations and decide if the emotions you are experiencing today are valid, or if they exist because you are reminded of something that affected you deeply in the past.

- Decide early in an emotionally charged situation if you are going to fight the situation, forget the situation, or reframe the situation.

If you decide to **fight** the situation, make sure it is worth the fight. You don't want to spend your time, money, energy, resources, and talent on ego-based "small stuff". If you decide to fight, you will need to put together a business case that identifies:

1. The present situation – the problem, issue, or challenge.
2. The ideal situation.
3. Barriers between the present situation and the ideal situation.
4. Options to explore in minimizing or eliminating the barriers.
5. The selection of the ideal option or solution.
6. Action to be taken to achieve success for you, the organization, or others involved in the situation.
7. The benefits or value of your ideas to the company, department, or people affected by the situation.
8. Your request for action.

If you decide to **forget** the situation, then you need to identify your reasons. This is important because as time goes by you might need to remind yourself of the reasons why you decided to forget the situation:

• Was it because the results would have not been worth the resources spent on the situation?
• The system was too contaminated?
• The people were too toxic?
• You didn't have the skills or the energy, or you had the skills and energy but you didn't have the time to address the situation?

Net it out. Become clear on why you are forgetting the situation, and then get busy and forget it.

If you decide to **reframe** the situation you need to decide how you can find middle ground so you can perform effectively. Reframing simply means lessening the negative points of a situation to where you can comfortably live with the situation. It might take the form of redirecting your thoughts or energy to areas where you get a greater personal and professional return.

Here's an example:
Suppose you dislike your job. You can:

1. Focus on how much you dislike your job and make it really miserable for yourself and those around you.

   OR

2. You can reframe by deciding what you can do to:
   - Make the job more enjoyable.
   - Make yourself more marketable so you can move on to another position in your company or in another company.

So ask yourself, procedurally, do you need to:

1. Revamp some processes in your job to make it more efficient?
2. Incorporate some new technologies to streamline the operation?
3. Negotiate with others to reduce some of the duplication of effort that might exist?

Personally, do you need to:

1. Make an attitude adjustment?
2. Readjust your thinking about people, processes, and performance standards.
3. Shore up your knowledge and skills so you can do a more effective and satisfying job?
4. Quit making your job performance suffer because things are not working in other areas of your life?
5. Spend time with upbeat, capable, and encouraging people who can coach and counsel you through this difficult time?
6. Develop a life outside of work.

Reframing often has to do with adjusting 20 percent or more of the situation so you can live with it comfortably. This means recognizing you might not be able to make the situation perfect, but you can make the situation more tolerable, workable, and less stressful.

Awareness Skills

Assertiveness

Assertiveness comes from understanding how we feel and think about people and events. It is demonstrated by our ability to state and support our feelings, thoughts, opinions or beliefs on a consistent basis.

Assertiveness is not to be confused with aggressiveness.

Aggressiveness is our need to force or impose upon others our feelings, thoughts, opinions, or beliefs. Assertiveness is more respectful. It enables both parties to maintain a sense of well-being, even when the other person has a different opinion from ours.

Assertiveness is about honoring ourselves. It is about putting our personal stake in the ground. When we are assertive, we are able to say, "I think, I feel, I need, I want, or I believe" in a way that is clear, concise, honest, and respectful.

If we are not comfortable talking in those terms, we need to learn. If we aren't prepared to take a position on people, places, or things, others will take a position for us and we might not like the end result. By then it's too late to start whining.

Emotionally Unaware options are to:

- Consistently ignore statements or actions by others that result in you feeling mad, sad, scared, shamed, disgusted, or surprised. By not speaking up when others do things that don't sit right with you, you reward poor performance. Indirectly, you give up control of your well-being to another person. And that does not demonstrate Emotional SMARTS!® Think about it. Who is going to look after your well-being if you don't?

- Take the position of not wanting to "cause trouble or make a fuss" because you hope the situation will blow over. Some things blow over – like clouds, hot air balloons, and kites. Most personal and interpersonal issues of substance don't blow over. Many times, unless you disclose your concerns and facilitate discussion, you can count on the fact they will blow up, not over!

- Live your life based on what you have been conditioned to think and do versus what you authentically think and want to do.

- If you live your life based on what you think you **SHOULD** do, versus what you really **WANT** to do or what you **WOULD** have done if the circumstances had been different, examine the power and influence of your family, your company, and friends on how you manage your life. It might be necessary to realign your priorities.

Demonstrating Emotional SMARTS!® means you:

- Learn how and when to say "No" – pleasantly, and in a way that allows both parties to save face.

- Take responsibility for protecting your emotional wellness. For example, you arrive late and leave early from people or places that are unhealthy for you to be around. Having said that, there are times where, for professional reasons, you need to make an appearance.

Consider this example: Your department (or family) is having a function that begins at 11 a.m. You know some people you are associated with do not party well. They tend to become belligerent or obnoxious, and this results in you feeling uncomfortable, unsafe, or isolated. You need to protect your well-being and also turn up at the function. Instead of arriving at 11 a.m. and staying until all the activities are over, you could arrive later in the day, around 2 or 3 p.m., and leave in the early evening. That way, you have been to the party, you have participated, and, most importantly, you have looked after your own wellness. You have not set yourself up to be set up!

- Learn to emotionally distance yourself from people or places where you are not able to shine. And, when you distance yourself, let go of those people and places with no animosity, no anger, bitterness, or hurt but with the greatest of ease and calmness. This will take work: journalling, counselling, praying, and time, but consider the words of comedian Buddy Hackett, "I've had a few arguments with people but I never carry a grudge. You know why? While you're carrying a grudge, they're out dancing."

- Become knowledgeable and skilled at making "I" statements. "I" statements are assertive statements you can make to another person when something they have said or done is causing you a problem.

Consider this example: A team member is consistently late for meetings and then, when she does arrive, she doesn't participate constructively. She nay-says, goes underground, and rather than quit and leave the meeting (or company), she quits and stays. Bottom line, she undermines the team-building process and company initiatives. Her behavior is consistently uncooperative and she provides little value to the work effort. Her behavior prevents team synergy, problem resolution, and fun building. An "I" message to her might sound like this:

1. **SET THE STAGE**

   Mary:

   I would like to speak with you about your involvement in our monthly meetings.

2. **REQUEST PERMISSION TO TALK**

   Is this a good time to talk?

   (If she says no – ask when would be a good time.)

3.   DESCRIBE THE BEHAVIOR

When you arrive at our monthly meetings late and participate by consistently opposing the ideas expressed by others in the department . . .

4.   DESCRIBE YOUR FEELINGS

I feel frustrated and annoyed . . .

5.   DESCRIBE THE RATIONALE FOR YOUR FEELINGS

because I want everyone in our meetings to be proactive, creative and results oriented.

(Be careful not to include the word "you" in this section because then the message becomes a blaming message.)

6.   SOLICIT FEEDBACK

What is the problem as you see it? OR What do you suggest we do about this? OR What do you think about what I have just said? OR What can we do to turn this situation around?

Very simply, you need to let the other person know his or her behavior is causing you a problem. You need to express how you feel about it, why you feel that way, and that you are willing to discuss the situation.

It's true, you cannot change other people, control their behaviors, nor solve their problems. By learning how to deliver "I" messages, however, you can ensure you are operating with Emotional SMARTS!® You will be clear, concise, honest, and respectful about what you need in the relationship.

Try an "I" message. Think of something about which you feel mad, sad, glad, scared, surprised, shamed, or disgusted, and create an "I" message in the following space.

Try the example below:

"I" Message Example

1.   SET THE STAGE:
I would like to speak with you about _____
_____

2.   PERMISSION TO TALK:
Is this a good time? _____
_____

3.   DESCRIBE THE BEHAVIOR:
When you said/did   _____
_____

4.   DESCRIBE YOUR FEELINGS:
I felt _____
_____

(Refer to the Feelings Vocabulary, pages 15-17, if you get stuck)

5.   DESCRIBE THE RATIONALE FOR YOUR FEELINGS:
because I   _____
_____

6.   SOLICIT FEEDBACK:
(What, How, Tell me) _____
_____

If you find it difficult to discuss a negative situation, create an "I" message for someone who has done something nice for you. An example might be acknowledging support you received from a co-worker. It might sound like this:

I would like to speak with you about how you helped me out last week.

Is this a good time?

When you went out of your way to help me with that proposal. . .

I was really appreciative . . .

because I had a number of things on my plate and it was getting to me.

Remember, "I" messages work for positive situations as well as negative situations. They can be an excellent way to reinforce, acknowledge and encourage positive behaviors of other people.

Don't be hesitant to use this powerful assertiveness communication skill. Remember, "I" messages are of value for you, as much as for the other person. They are vehicles for you to use to stand up for yourself, to establish boundaries in your relationships, and to help others learn how to treat you. If you don't teach people how to treat you, they will make up their own rules about how to treat you, and that might not work very well from your perspective.

On the negative side, if people want to prove to you that they have low flexibility, low self-regard, and low emotional intelligence, they will respond to your "I" message negatively or defensively. They might say: "Tell someone who cares. So what. That's your problem, not mine, so what am I suppose to do about it?" If they have that reaction, and you are demonstrating the Emotional SMARTS!® of emotional self-awareness, self-management, assertiveness, and optimism, the good news is that you get to practice sending them another "I" message!

And consider this, if you consistently receive negative feedback and invalidation from the people in your life, you need to ask yourself why you think so little of yourself that you would accept that behavior. You need to get serious about understanding why you stay in a personal or professional relationship with someone who treats you with disregard, disrespect, or disdain.

Awareness Skills

Goal Achievement

Goal achievement is our ability to consistently identify, describe, and pursue things that help us honor ourselves and realize our potential. When we work towards goals, or specific areas of interest to us, we become self-actualized – the best we can be! We are motivated to do what we need to do to make good things happen for us. We consciously and unconsciously seek out people and situations that facilitate achieving our goals.

Think about this. It is hard for us to identify, describe, and pursue things that are important to us if we are unable to identify our feelings and assertively describe what we want to do or have. Using one Emotional SMARTS!® characteristic builds on the next. We are better able to stay motivated in achieving our goals if we can identify our feelings (emotional self-awareness), manage our emotions to support our actions (emotional management), and describe our needs, wants, and "nice to haves" to ourselves and others (assertiveness).

Goal achievement provides an opportunity for us to demonstrate our personal courage, our knowledge, skill, and staying power. It is an opportunity for us to be accountable, if to no one else but ourselves. Goal achievement does not always have to relate to large external issues such as learning four new software programs by the end of the year. It can be as simple as committing to take a walk around the block each lunch hour in order to lessen your stress level. Or, if you are a workaholic, to leave the office 15 minutes early each day in order to have 15 more minutes with your children, partner, or self.

People who write out their goals have a better chance of achieving what is important to them. (You may want to use a journal or copy book for this portion – your goals and concerns will likely change over time, particularly as you develop your Emotional SMARTS!®)

Consider what you want in your life from these areas:

1. Emotional health

2. Physical health

3. Spiritual wellness

4. Family and intimate relationships

5. Friends and social relationships

6. Career and work opportunities

7. Financial status

8. Overall quality of life

9. _____

10. _____

11. _____

12. _____

Now identify areas where you would like to see improvement in your life. Let's take the example of getting more exercise.

1. **Specifically state your goal.**

   I want to exercise at least 30 minutes per day, 5 days a week.

2. **When will you start the process of meeting your goal?**

   Today.

3. **What are the benefits of meeting your goal? (What's in it for you?)**

   Feel good, lose weight, firm up, more energy, better attitude.

4. **What might hold you back from meeting your goal?**

   Work commitments, family commitments, feeling tired, no routine, hate it – not fun.

5. **What can you do to lessen the intensity of the "hold back" issues?**

    Schedule an appointment at a certain time each day; exercise with a buddy; use some stimulating music to exercise by; reward yourself each week with a non-food item; buy a mirror that makes you look skinny . . .

6. **How will you stay motivated when the going gets tough?**

    Look at a "fit" picture; talk to a pal; make your exercise time more than just an exercise period, make it an exercise and creative thinking time; find something fun to do; vary your activity and routine; get up early, get moving, and get it over with.

7. **How will you measure your success?**

    Weight loss; lower blood pressure; clothes fit more comfortably; track your performance in a journal; feedback from others on how you look and behave.

Emotionally Unaware responses could be to:

- Expect the government, an employer, a friend, a significant other, or a partner to meet your wants and needs. As the song says, it is important not to look for love in all the wrong places. Emotional SMARTS!® does not allow alternate sources to look after you and what is important to you. Only you can be responsible for your psychological well-being, your career, your relationships, your health, and your finances.

  Should it happen that other sources help you with your initiatives, terrific, but don't count on it and then you won't fall into the entitlement trap. Entitlement is a name given to an attitude when people expect things they have not worked for or earned. People with entitlement attitudes are often mad, sad, scared, surprised, shamed, or disgusted when things don't work out the way they anticipated. People with entitlement attitudes often name, blame, and shame others for their own lack of success.

People with entitlement attitudes often come from a mindset of "lesser than". In this mindset, nothing is ever right enough, good enough, fast enough, or cheap enough. The opposite of this attitude is that of being "better than". With this attitude people feel and act superior to those around them. In both cases, people do and say things that alienate others.

A more emotionally smart mindset is that of being "equal to". With this mindset we believe and act as though our wants, needs, and rights are as important as the next person's. We are equal to others and therefore behave in a way that facilitates collaboration and cooperation.

- Not identifying what is important to you in the major aspects of your life. If you don't have an image of what is important to you, how do you intend to measure your success? How will you know if you are winning and, equally as important, how will you know if you are losing?

- Consistently work for free or not take your earned holidays.

When you consistently work and are not renumerated for it, you send a message to yourself and others that your intellectual, physical, and emotional capital are not important. You are really saying your performance and contribution aren't of value. Now, I'm not talking here about volunteering – that's different. Volunteering is what you choose to do to give back to your community. I'm also not talking about occasionally working early or late to complete an important project – that's called having a good attitude and work ethic.

What I refer to now is when people consistently work unremunerated hours, above and beyond their normal work agreement, or when they do not take earned holidays. This well-intentioned act often creates a disservice to the organization, because these actions project a distorted and incorrect picture of what it takes to run the business from both a human, capital, and resource perspective.

Using your Emotional SMARTS!® means you:

- Set goals in each area of importance to you and chart your progress on a regular basis.

- Join groups or organizations that help you develop knowledge and skills in the areas that are important to you. If you want to be a better communicator, join a public speaking group. If you want to learn how to invest, join an investment club; join the Chamber of Commerce, Board of Trade, or community-oriented service groups if you want to learn about new careers or work opportunities. Along with what you learn, you will meet people who can help you make your goals a reality.

Goal Achievement is exciting. When you see yourself making progress on things that are important to you, your self-esteem builds. The academic word for this behavior is self-efficacy. Self-efficacy means that as you take on new challenges and accomplish what is important to you, your sense of well-being increases. The more you are able to do, the more you are capable of, and the better you feel about yourself. The better you feel about yourself, the better you feel about other people and situations. As you feel better about your business and personal relationships, you tend to be more optimistic, effective, and resilient in other aspects of your life.

Awareness Skills

Optimism

Optimism is our ability to maintain a positive outlook on life. When we are optimistic, we find the "lesson" in everything that happens – the good, the bad, and the mediocre.

If something good happens, we are grateful. We ask ourselves, "What we are doing right that gives us such good results?" We incorporate these same actions and attitudes in the next similar situation. We give thanks for our ongoing success.

If something unfortunate happens, we ask what lessons we need to learn from the experience. What are we doing that gives us such a bad result? What do we need to do next time to prevent another bad outcome? Let's put a plan in place so we don't repeat unproductive and ineffective actions.

(Let's face it – most of us learn more from the bad times than we do from the good times, so even the bad times have some benefit to them, and when we are emotionally smart we recognize that.)

When something mediocre happens, we consciously identify what needs to be done to create a more positive outcome. How can we do it better the next time?

Emotionally Unaware behaviors in the optimism department are:

- Naming, blaming, or shaming others because life and work outcomes do not measure up to your expectations.

- Not giving credit where credit is due.

- Putting down people, places, or things that appear to be positive, performing, and progressive.

Emotional SMARTS!® means you get to:

- Say please and thank you to your higher power, your God, and to other people. Tell them what they did that made a difference to you, and why it made a difference.

- Give one compliment, one supportive statement, or an encouraging word to at least one person each day.

- Work hard not to say no, won't, can't, never, and that's not my job. These are "go nowhere" statements and they can quickly label you as having a bad attitude.

- Acknowledge a difficult situation with another person, particularly if you are worried or anxious about the situation three days after it happened. A rule of thumb that can keep you operating in a grounded and centered way is if a situation is still on your mind or in your heart three days after it happened, You Own It! It won't be going away. You need to identify, acknowledge, and process the feelings that go along with it by acknowledging the difficult situation with the person most directly affected, with a trusted friend, or with yourself. This will lessen the negative intensity of the event and limit its draining undercurrent in your life.

- Limit your time with negative, blaming, or whining people. They have the potential to drain you of your energy, your enthusiasm, and your Emotional SMARTS! After you have made an effort to resolve negativity with another person, if it can't be done or you don't see hope in the situation, take responsibility for your "stuff" so you can move up and out. Make sure you take with you only what is yours. Don't assume responsibility for the other person's "stuff". (Yours will probably keep you busy enough!) You can only move on with optimism when you deal with your issues and take your power back from those who might use and abuse it.

- Work out – go for a walk, hop on a treadmill, lift some weights, sign up for a yoga class, or dance around your living room.

- Read positive affirmations, spiritual readings, special quotations, or mottos that help you remain encouraged about your performance in life. One saying that kept me going through the dark and difficult days of my doctoral degree was, "The strongest steel is forged by the hottest fire". Another was a wonderful graphic of two penguins facing each other. One penguin has a big fish over his head that is trying to swallow him whole. The caption at the top of the graphic is "Relax, God's in charge". I found that graphic settled me down when I became emotionally charged over certain academic decisions. Today I still have that picture taped to my computer.

- Practice being optimistic. Optimistic people are perceived as resilient. They weather life's challenges well. They recover quickly and carry on with a sense of direction and a positive attitude. As a result, they are seen as encouraging in spirit, promising in performance, and rewarding to be around.

C H A P T E R   2

BEHAVIORAL SKILLS

Behavioral skills relate to our ability to operate free of emotional dependency on others, to monitor our stress reactions, to control our impulses and delay immediate gratification in order to achieve longer term wants or needs, and to manage conflict with others.

Self-Reliance

Stress Management

Impulse Control

Conflict Management

Behavioral Skills

Self-Reliance

Self-reliance is our ability to depend on ourselves to make things happen. When we are self-reliant, we rely on our own capabilities, judgments, and resources. We conduct our lives free of emotional dependency on another person, a company, or our environment.

That is not to say we do things with no consideration of others. We honor ourselves and others in ways that are ethical, legal, and culturally appropriate. We do things based on our wants, needs, beliefs, values, goals, and aspirations without getting caught up in a cycle of needing constant approval or endorsement from others.

Be Aware! Sometimes, when we try to break away from people or places that are unhealthy for us to be around, some people try to sabotage, invalidate, or undermine us. They do this because they want to maintain control over their environment and we happen to be part of that environment. People who demonstrate a pronounced desire to control us need us in their lives to validate themselves. We can lessen their negative influence on our well-being by demonstrating our own good AWARENESS skills.

If we understand our feelings in the situation (self-awareness), if we are able to manage our emotions and stand our ground (emotion management), if we are able to state our position in a clear, concise, honest, and non-judgmental manner (assertiveness), if we are able to stay focused on our goal(s) (goal achievement) and if we are able to see the bright side of everything that happens to us (optimism), we are better able to deal with the people who want to put us down, pull us back, or push us under.

When we operate with an independent and positive spirit, we attract people to us and frequent places of work and play where our uniqueness is valued, positively challenged and rewarded.

Emotionally Unaware aspects of self-reliance can be to:

- Live your life and make decisions based on what you think other people want you to do. This is a sure way to drive yourself crazy because with some people you will seldom measure up to what they expect of you. And, even if you did measure up they wouldn't be able to let you know you had. This would happen more because of where they are at than because of what you have done.

- Be fearful of another person's reactions to your decisions and, therefore, not make decisions that will positively affect your well-being. If you let the fear rule, you give your personal power away. Giving your power away diminishes your well-being and your level of self-esteem and assertiveness. It also sets you up to feel and act victimized and needy.

- Expect your partner, your company, a union, or the government to look after any aspect of your life. If you adopt an independent attitude that reinforces that you are responsible for your overall well-being and life results, should your partner, your company, or the government come through with things that add value to your life – that is a bonus, not a right!

- Bask in the reflected glory of who you work for, live with, are friends with, or married to. Reflected glory is when we try to build our self worth on someone else's achievements. Pride in another person's accomplishments is one thing, trying to gain your self worth from them is another.

Emotional SMARTS!® means you adopt personal independence to:

• Identify what you want, need, desire, think, and hope for, so you make decisions and choices that facilitate what is important to you.

  Now, before you think this is a selfish way to behave, consider that many people have, in the past, put their company first, their family or relationship next, and themselves last to no avail. The problem with this approach is, when environmental change happens, people have little to fall back on. They have lost their self-identity. This happens because they spent all their energy elsewhere – looking after the company, their family, or their relationship issues and they have little or nothing left for themselves.

  Another, more realistic, approach for today's workplace is to put yourself first, your family or relationship next, and the company last. That might sound like an uncaring and disloyal way to behave, but it isn't. Consider this, if you look after yourself and constantly strive to operate with all your Emotional SMARTS!® then you are better able to honor yourself and to carry out family and relationship commitments. If you are feeling good about yourself and good about your relationships, you are better able to look after company issues. Why? Because if you feel good about who you are and what you are doing, and you are surrounded by healthy people and environments, you will be more likely to approach work with an attitude of optimism and a "can do" spirit.

• Constantly learn new skills and develop new competencies so you can be current and involved in varied, stimulating, and cutting edge activities. It will keep you active, interested, and interesting. It will also make you "marketable" should the need arise for you to seek other opportunities, either in or outside your organization.

Behavioral Skills

Stress Management

Stress comes in three flavors:

Stress

Distress

Eustress

Stress is a nonspecific response of the body to demands made upon it. It sounds pretty clinical, but all it really means is our bodies react to changes in our work or our relationships in very predictable ways.

For example, you learned this afternoon that your company was just purchased by another organization. The information acts as a stressor. If you are then questioned about your position, your responsibilities, or your performance, and the questions cause you to feel scared or vulnerable, you are exhibiting a stress reaction. If you go home tonight and are unable to sleep because you feel anxious about why the questions are being asked, how you are perceived, or what might happen to you in the new organization, your insomnia is also a stress reaction.

Stress becomes **distress** when it causes damage to us. Distress is when we react intensely to situations by overreacting. For example, we might not be able to sleep; we might overeat or not eat at all; we might emotionally act out by yelling, crying, or withdrawing.

When we intensely react over the long term to a number of different issues, our bodies will show us who is boss and will talk back to us by becoming sick, tired, listless, or dead.

Eustress, on a happier note, is something that challenges us to get moving. An example might be notification that you have a chance to take on a new job, in a new department, in the new organization. That could prompt you to ready your resumé, learn a new software program, drop ten pounds, or start a workout regimen.

Emotionally Unaware responses to managing stress are to:

- *Over-anything!* Over-react, over-eat, over-drink, over-spend, over-exercise, over-work, over-analyze,

  OR

- *Under-anything!* Withdraw, hide out, procrastinate, or emotionally shut down.

- Attempt to escape the situation through the use of or addictions to drugs, gambling, alcohol, or sexual encounters.

- Try and control the situation through verbal abuse or passive or aggressive (violent) behavior.

Stress management techniques that display Emotional SMARTS!® **are to:**

- Take control. Find a trusted friend, advisor, or mentor to talk to about the situation and then build a plan to take action and exert control over your issues.

- Get some exercise that results in your heart rate beating faster than it does than when sitting at your desk. Studies prove that exercise, done properly, releases happy little chemical reactions in your brain called endorphins. Endorphins physically change how your body and mind react to stressful situations. Endorphins are not to be underestimated – they can change your physical and emotional reaction to stress.

- Write down your situation in a journal or diary. Write a letter to the individual who helped to create your stressful situation. Tell him or her exactly what you think and how you feel. Then do not, repeat DO NOT, mail the letter. Put it away in a private spot; read it regularly; add to it when necessary; and when the situation has lessened in its emotional intensity, shred, tear up or burn the letter, and throw it away.

- Create something. Plant flowers; paint pictures; write stories; take pictures; build crafts; build projects; bake goodies; cook meals for a homeless shelter.

- Get active. Visit a senior's lodge; hug a child; hug a pet; clean closets, desks, garages, or the refrigerator; polish shoes; take a walk; go to the zoo.

- Get inactive. Give yourself permission to hunker down; put fresh sheets on the bed and stay there all day or all week-end. Don't answer your telephone, fax machine, or e-mail. Remember it will all be there for you to deal with when you have restored your spirit. Don't do anything you don't want to do and, best of all, **don't feel guilty!**

- Remember the "HALT" theory. Protect yourself and pay particular attention to how you are self-managing, behaving, connecting with others, and making decisions when you are **H**ungry, **A**ngry, **L**onely, or **T**ired. The more you are affected by those dynamics, the more important it is for you to be diligent in managing your Emotional SMARTS!®

Behavioral Skills

Impulse Control

Impulse control is a significant factor in demonstrating our emotional intelligence competence. Impulse control is our ability to resist temptations, drives, or intense impulses to say or do something that might negatively affect us in the future.

On the dark side, lack of impulse control is often at the very foundation of society's ills: domestic violence; elder, child, or animal abuse; road, air, technology, and office rage. These events take place because people are unable to control their intense emotions, and they are overtaken by the need to act out and take action, or act in, withdraw or go "underground" with their behaviors.

On a lighter note, the lack of impulse control can show itself in starting a diet on Monday, only to have the gratification of intense impulses take over by Wednesday! In short, when we experience an intense emotional reaction to a situation where we want to act or speak with no thought about the ramifications of our action, that is exactly the time we need to give ourselves the gifts of time and thought – we need to work hard to control our impulses!

In time, we might well say what we want to say, or do what we want to do, however, with time and thought on our side, we might approach the situation with a more balanced perspective, and less emotionally charged words.

Emotionally Unaware responses that demonstrate poor impulse control are:

• Sending any type of correspondence, a letter, e-mail, or phone mail message, when you are upset or frustrated by an issue or another person's behavior. Remember, you don't ever want to put anything in writing that you would be embarrassed to have read in a courtroom.

- Medicating yourself by attempting to purchase your way to calmness. Consistently buying things you can't afford, don't need, or don't enjoy just because it's Thursday or . . .

- Telling people "off" because you are fearful, frustrated, and fatigued in your life, work, and relationships.

- Threatening people with harsh, intense statements and actions that negatively affect their sense of safety and well-being, and your reputation.

When you control your impulses using your Emotional SMARTS!® you are able to:

- Self-manage by immediately controlling the urge to act out (where you say or do something you might regret), or act in (where you go "underground" and attempt to maintain control of people and the environment you are in by withdrawing).

- Saying "No, thank you" to people or things that could injure or harm your positive sense of self, your well-being, or the well-being of others you care about.

- Learn phrases that help you gain the time you need to make an informed decision. Phrases like:

    "I need some time to think this through."
    "Let me consider this for a day (a while, the week-end . . .)."
    "I'd like to check out how this will fit with the other plans."

These phrases can give you a sense of control over a situation when you might feel vulnerable and unsafe. They also help to give you time to ask questions; time to reflect on the answers; time to consider other influencing factors and not feel as though your back is to the wall to make an immediate decision. Having a sense of control over your behavior contributes to your self-management, assertiveness, optimism, independence, and stress management.

Look at the big, long-term picture and assess the situation by asking, "Could this situation cost me . . ."

Time?

Money?

Energy?

My health?

A reputation and some credibility (mine or someone else's)?

OR a Relationship?

Because, if it is going to cost you something, you need the gifts of time and thought – time to think, assess, and decide whether or not you want to proceed with your initial reaction to the situation – thought to become grounded, centered, and focused. You need to do what many people were told to do as children: count to 10; walk around the block; talk to your spiritual advisor; sleep on it. Your skill at controlling your intense impulses will speak volumes about your ability to build, manage, and demonstrate your Emotional SMARTS!®

Behavioral Skills

Conflict Management

The potential for conflict is all around us. Unfortunately, not many of us have been educated and socialized on how to work through conflict. When we experience conflict, it could be over differing styles (how we behave), values (what we believe), expectations (what we hope for), or our interpretation of the information.

When faced with differing styles, values, or expectations, a survival instinct is to adopt one of three behavior patterns:

Fight

Flight

Freeze

If we choose the **fight** behavior pattern, we will quickly, intently, and without thinking respond to an emotionally charged situation If we use this pattern on a consistent basis, over the long term, it can result in our being perceived as inappropriately aggressive, intensely angry, paranoid or out of control.

If, on the other hand, we consistently take a **flight** behavior pattern with conflict, we will withdraw, pull back, ignore, and try to distance ourselves from the situation. In this instance, people could think we are insensitive, uncaring, or incompetent in proactively addressing difficult situations.

If we **freeze**, we will be immobilized mentally, physically, and emotionally over the long term. In this case, we simply shut down and feel unable, de-energized, and de-motivated to take action on the situation we are facing. If we "freeze" on a consistent basis when faced with challenging situations, it could result in people questioning our capabilities in terms of our ability to be personally responsible, accountable, and competent in resiliently responding to life and work challenges.

Each of these approaches has value – they are not always negative or inappropriate. There are times when the best behavior would be to have a "fight" pattern. On the other hand, there are times when this behavioral pattern could be inappropriate for the situation, the people involved in the situation, and the culture of the environment.

As well, there are times when there is merit to taking "flight" and withdrawing from a situation so you have time to assess, think, reflect, and plan how you are going to address the challenge. A key consideration here is whether you take "flight" in all, or most challenging situations, and whether your approach is used to keep yourself as safe as possible rather than attempting to find a solutions that people can comfortably live with.

"Freezing" can have merit in that it can isolate us from a situation long enough for us to recover emotionally, gain inner strength, knowledge, and skill on how to get started in productively addressing the conflict. Should it happen that we "freeze" over the long term, and make no effort to become competent in addressing our situation, others might perceive us as ineffective or "high maintenance".

We need to identify our preferred conflict management style. Then, we need to ask ourselves if, on a consistent basis when we are faced with conflict or interpersonal challenges, we are using the best possible approach for the situation, the people involved, and the cultural environment.

In today's intense and fast-paced interpersonal workplace, learning to manage behaviors so you can **fight**, take **flight** or appropriately **freeze** during conflict is a powerful business skill. That is where impulse control skills and other emotionally smart characteristics come into play. People who are willing to appropriately address conflict situations are better able to gain support from others and ultimately resolve difficult situations.

Emotionally Unaware conflict responses could be to:
- Physically strike a person or animal.
- Verbally abuse another person. A common verbal abuse technique is when a person divides, conquers, and invalidates something that he or she doesn't have, understand, or feel comfortable with.

For example, in your efforts to increase your emotional intelligence, you start taking courses on topics that will increase your relationship effectiveness. You attend a non-technical, interpersonal-skills type of workshop, and when you return to the office you tell your associates about your positive learning experience.

If someone in your group was to divide, conquer, and invalidate you after you had made positive comments on the learning experience, it might sound like this:

1. **Divide**:   Hey, did you go to that hug-in session last week? OR
                  Don't tell me you attended that kissy-face course! OR
                  Did you really go to that love-in deal by HR?

2. **Conquer:**   That stuff is just another flavor of the month   OR
                  Here we go with another management fad!   OR
                  Yeah, more of that touchy feeling nonsense!

3. **Invalidate:** You'll do anything to get a free lunch   OR
                  You'd do anything to not have to work   OR
                  It's amazing what you'll do for a day off

The bottom line of this inappropriate and often-used technique is that it incorporates name-calling, labeling, or ridiculing of another person. In my experience, these types of comments say more about the person saying them than they do about the person receiving them.

We often reward this type of behavior by not addressing the situation, and by doing so we send a subtle message of endorsement to the other person by not addressing what they said and how they said it. Very simply, we reward their inappropriate behavior by not speaking up and out about what they said, how we feel about it, and why we feel that way.

Giving someone free rein to continue with these types of comments can result in an individual becoming the resident corporate or family bully, where all that has changed since their days on the playground is that now they operate in an office or home environment.

If you don't apply your Emotional SMARTS!® around this type of behavior, you could be the loser because you will let their low Emotional SMARTS!® diminish your sense of enlightenment, well-being, and accomplishment.

Emotional SMARTS!® help you to manage conflict by allowing you to:

- Be aware of your preferred instinctual conflict-management style. Is it fight, flight, or freeze? You need to know this so you can self-manage when your instinctive response wants to take over inappropriately.

- Identify how your instinctive behavioral style benefits you or how it lessens your influence, effectiveness, and endorsement by others.

- Not spend your valuable time, energy, or money trying to fix unfixable people, places, or situations.

- Not become a voluntary victim. If you are in a situation, either personal or professional, that causes you anger, anxiety, frustration, discontent, or unhappiness approximately 80 percent of the time or more, you need to take charge of your Emotional SMARTS!® You need to ask yourself what you are doing to contribute to the situation and what you can do to either reframe the situation so you can comfortably live with it or forget it so you can move on with honoring yourself.

C H A P T E R 3

CONTACT SKILLS

Contact skills refer to our ability to build and maintain durable, empathetic relationships with a range of people, and to support those who are less fortunate, and the common values of our society and environment.

Relationship Building

Empathy

Community Care

Contact Skills

Relationship Building

Most people want to live and work with people who are likeable, trustworthy, and capable. Likeable in terms of being easy to respect, encouraging in attitude, and safe to be around. Trustworthy in terms of being authentic, honest, ethical, and fair. Capable in terms of being knowledgeable, skilled, and competent in being our leader, friend, partner, sister, brother, parent, grandparent, or family member. We need to remember this as we present ourselves at work, at home, and in our community activities, because if that is what we would like from others, we need to ensure we are doing our best to be respected or liked, trusted, and capable, with those with whom we work and live.

Effective relationship-building skills result in the establishment of diverse, mutually beneficial relationships in all aspects of our lives. People who have effective relationship-building skills enjoy long-term relationships that benefit them personally and professionally.

In business, benefits of effective relationship-building skills relate to career advancement, credibility in the business community, recognition, influence, and increased financial rewards. In personal situations, benefits relate to relationships of trust, intimacy, safety, and fun.

Emotionally Unaware skills that have a negative impact on your relationship-building skills are to:

- Take people for granted and not pay attention to how you treat and serve your customers, suppliers, employees, family, and friends.

- Not give back . . . Not return telephone calls, not send thank-you notes, or not let other people know that you appreciate what they do in, and for, your relationship.

- Not disclose what you hope for in a relationship and what is important to you in maintaining that relationship. Consistent lack of openness and appropriate disclosure creates feelings of apprehension and mistrust. Over time, lack of disclosure can result in the death of a relationship. The reason it dies is because there is no future focus, no commonality, and no sense of connection.

- Have a cast of thousands as your "best friends". You cannot be all things to all people. When you are not selective about how you spend your time and with whom you spend it, you can spread yourself so thin that there is no energy or time left for you to recharge and refocus on the relationships that are important to you. Over time, those important relationships dissolve because the people in them don't think they matter.

- Make contact with people only when you need something. Remember, the time to build and nurture a relationship is when you don't need anything from the relationship.

Emotional SMARTS!® lets you build healthy relationships because you know how to:

- Let people know when they have done nice things for you. Write notes, make telephone calls, send treats, or "I like you" messages. This does not have to be expensive, time consuming, or embarrassing. It can be as simple as saying, "Hey, I really enjoyed our visit. I like your spirit and enthusiasm. I'm glad you're my pal. I learn from you and I like that. And, Thank you."

- Try to meet and get to know at least one new person, either professionally or personally, on a regular basis. Putting forth effort to know people from various walks of life is as important as knowing your job. The time to build relationships is when you don't need them. Then . . . they are there when you do!

- Listen. Listen not only to the words being used by the other person, but listen to how they feel about the topic being discussed.

- Keep your word. If you can't, let those most affected know why you can't and what you plan to do about it. Do this sooner versus later.

- Help people learn. When you come across material that is in their field of interest, send it to them. If you are in a position to mentor or coach others, share your experiences, empathy, and business acumen. It helps others to feel less isolated and more encouraged.

- Help people work. Refer people you believe in to work opportunities or positive visibility.

- Help people win. Use local people and services whenever possible. If necessary, educate and coach them on what they need to do to be world class. Why not support your own!

Empathy

Empathy is a core characteristic of Emotional SMARTS!® Empathy does not mean agreement or sympathy. Empathy is when we are able to acknowledge another person's thoughts, feelings, or actions, particularly in emotionally charged situations. It doesn't mean we know exactly how they feel, because if we haven't had the exact experience, we won't know their specific feelings. We can understand and appreciate, however, they are experiencing strong emotions about what is happening to or around them.

An example might be: A single parent arrives at work on Monday morning having been at the hospital all weekend with a sick child. The parent arrives at work tired and worried, but he or she comes because an important report is due to be sent to head office that day.

A colleague might demonstrate empathy by saying "It must be very worrisome for you right now. Is there anything I can do to give you a hand?"

Another example might be: A colleague is feeling the effects of numerous organizational changes and is withdrawing and becoming distant with you and the rest of the team. An empathic statement might be:

"You seem discouraged these days. If you want to talk about things, I'm open to listening."

When demonstrating empathy, we don't have to solve other people's problems, fix anything, or become a psychologist. We are simply acknowledging the feelings they might have about the situation we believe they are experiencing. We are willing to let them know we are willing to hear them – not just listen to their words, but hear the emotions behind their words.

The worst thing that can happen is that you identify an emotion they are not feeling. In most cases, they will simply correct you and keep talking. For example, if you had a colleague who was acting out and being aggressive because of being told he or she needed to work on the long weekend, you might say "You must be disappointed about having to work this weekend". If he or she weren't disappointed, but were angry, it is likely the response would be: "No, I'm not disappointed, I am really ticked off that things aren't more organized around this place." A key point here is that the emotionally charged person is "venting". That is positive – they are releasing pent up energy about the situation.

An important aspect in demonstrating empathy is one's spirit of intent. It will quickly become apparent to the other person if we are sincere in our efforts to acknowledge their feelings. The other person will feel "heard", recognized, and valued, and we all know how we feel when someone creates that environment for us.

Emotionally Unaware, non-empathetic responses are to:

- Think that empathy is a lightweight trait and doesn't matter. Many a transaction, interview, sale, or relationship has been lost because one person didn't feel heard, valued, understood, or appreciated.

- Try to appear empathic when you really don't care about the person or their situation. That translates to insincerity and most people see that deception coming a mile away.

Empathy, when you employ your Emotional SMARTS!®, means you are able to:

- Identify your feelings. The better you are at identifying your feelings, the more effective you will be at identifying the feelings of others through their language, facial expression, tone of voice, and body language.

- Practice identifying the feelings of others. Let people know you sense where they are coming from. Empathy could sound like this:

> It sounds like you are OVERWHELMED with what is going on.

> You seem RELIEVED the decision has been made.

> You appear DISCOURAGED about the changes at work.

> I think you are ENCOURAGED about the new job opportunity.

The ability to authentically demonstrate empathy is a powerful skill in any relationship. If you think this is an area where you need practice, the next time you are listening to someone discuss an emotionally charged event, ask yourself: "If I was that person, experiencing that event, how would I feel?" Then, consider whether you would be mad, sad, glad, scared, feeling surprise, shame, disgust, or love. When you have identified how you might feel, send that message back to the other party and see what happens. Don't be surprised if how you feel is very similar to how they feel. By letting them know you are willing to discuss the facts of the situation, along with the emotional side of it, you send a message of being approachable, human, and "real".

Contact Skills

Community Care

Community care means we actively contribute to the well-being of our community. Community care or social responsibility, can take many different forms in our home, work, relationship, or social groups.

People with a sense of community care are responsible and participative citizens. When we support social values in our community and seek to join with others who respect social guidelines, we demonstrate our understanding and willingness to contribute to more than just our immediate world. Through our participating, volunteering, donating time, energy, expertise, talent, or money, we support our community and help forge stronger interpersonal connections.

Emotionally Unaware attitudes to community care are to:

- Park in handicapped areas when you are not handicapped.

- Bully, beat up or abuse people or animals.

- Abuse our environment by discarding trash or toxic material anywhere other than a trash can or proper disposal unit. Consider this: What if everyone dumped their garbage wherever they wanted? What kind of an example would that set and what kind of an environment would it create?

**Social responsibility means you use your Emotional SMARTS!®
to:**

- Reduce, recycle or reuse things wherever possible.

- Live with a consciousness of being moral, ethical, and respectful of society's norms, values and standards.

C H A P T E R 4

DECISION-MAKING SKILLS

Decision-making skills refer to our ability to proactively identify potential challenges and creatively select solutions that are
specific, measurable, attainable, results-oriented, and timely.

Problem Identification

Creativity

Selecting Solutions

Reality Testing

Decision-Making Skills

Problem Identification

In order to be effective decision makers, we have to be able to identify potential problems before they become large problems. We need to be able to identify issues that could potentially cost us time, money, energy, health, our reputation, credibility, or a relationship. People who are skilled at problem identification conduct their life with a "what if?" attitude, without obsessing about issues. They think about the impact of events taking place around them. They don't feel overwhelmed, frantic, rushed, doomed, pressured, or anxious about issues. They appear to address problems with a sense of calm, control, and competence.

Emotionally Unaware things to do here are:

- Not prepare and keep current a résumé or business profile. Having one that is current is not a sign of disloyalty. In today's fragile and ever-changing workplace, it's a sign that you understand the realities of the day and are prepared to apply for positions, both internal or external to your organization, where your knowledge and skills can be best used.

- Not prepare yourself to learn, develop, change and prosper. Look three to five years down the road; your actions today are the basis for your results tomorrow.

Emotional SMARTS!® let you identify problems because of your ability to:

- Think beyond the present situation and identify specific actions to take to address a problem situation over the long term, and then assess the probable outcomes as a result of your actions.

- Become skilled in thinking about cause and effect.

For example: As you deal with life issues, ask yourself, "If I do this, what will be the effect or consequence of my decision?"

Ask "Who? What? When? Where? How? Why? and How Much?" types of questions as they help identify the scope and depth of issues.

For example: If you think you would like to change jobs, prior to leaving your existing position, you need to ask yourself questions such as:

1. What skills do I have that make me marketable, both internally and externally, to a company?

2. What makes me different or unique from other people in the same field?

3. Who else might I be able to work for within my existing company?

4. Who could use my services outside of this organization?

5. Where could I make the best contribution and be the happiest?

6. When should I make the decision to leave this position?

7. How would I go about getting a new position?

8. Why am I considering this move?

9. How much will this move cost me in terms of time, money, energy, or relationships?

10. How old will I be in five years if I do this? How old will I be in five years if I don't?

11. What is the worst thing that could happen to me if I do this? What will I do about it if it does?

12. What is the best thing that could happen to me if I do this?

People who are able to effectively identify potential problems keep themselves out of negative high-stress situations because they anticipate and prepare for the best and the worst of the situation prior to the situation unfolding.

Decision-Making Skills

Creativity

Creativity is our ability to identify and explore a variety of approaches or solutions in our quest to address problems that arise in life. When we are creative, we are willing to consider other ideas, options, and possible outcomes. We behave in a way that indicates we are flexible and versatile.

Our behavioral style – the way we say and do things – affects our creativity. Each of the four main behavioral styles discussed in this chapter places a different value on time, desired results, risk taking, people issues, processes or procedures. Being creative takes time, effort and a willingness to take risks as we explore various options, approaches, and outcomes related to our situation. Different behavioral styles demonstrate their creativity differently.

For example, some people place a high value on facts and data and, as a result, they place a high value on the task or job to be done. Others place a high value on people and seek to establish a relationship with others prior to proceeding with the task at hand. Some people move, speak, and process information quickly – time has a high value to this group. Others prefer to be more methodical and will evaluate all aspects of communication, from movement, speech, and information processing, prior to saying or doing anything that commits them.

There is no one right or wrong style. We all demonstrate some characteristics of each style. The point is, we have a primary style that affects our behavior, expectations, and interactions with others. We also have a secondary style that we revert to when our corporate and personal needs are not being met, or our values are being violated.

There are four primary styles, each with particular characteristics that bring strengths and weaknesses to the work group and workplace. The more flexible each style is, the better the group or organization will function. Workplaces with a balance of all four styles, that operate with flexibility, become creative communities because it is in this diversity that old patterns are evaluated in terms of relevance and results. In such an environment, new patterns are given the opportunity to bloom and questionable patterns are questioned.

The chart, description and Quick Reference Style Guide at the end of this chapter explains a style guide which, I believe, belongs inside every business portfolio and on every refrigerator door in the country. (Don't all important documents end up on the refrigerator door?)

The chart is a quick reference guide that highlights the important characteristics of each style. You will notice on the chart I have used two descriptive titles for each style type. The reason for this is because these terms are often used interchangeably.

While this chart does not capture all characteristics of each style, it is intended to highlight major characteristics, wants, needs and values of each style. The charts explain what motivates people within a particular style, on a corporate and personal level, to do and say the things they do. It also identifies what people value, their particular behavioral patterns, and their normal reactions when they get cranky. And, it describes the actions you can take to lessen a partner's, co-worker's or friend's tension (or crankiness) to support the relationship, so you both can move on with the task at hand.

It is important to know the key characteristics of the four behavioral styles to be able to identify your preferred style and the style of those people with whom you come in contact. Understanding the various styles gives you insight into how to highlight the best in yourself and bring out the best in others, so you end up with the most creative, timely, people-sensitive, and results-oriented solutions.

The four primary styles are:

The Dominant or Driver

The Influencer or Expressive

The Steadier or Amiable

The Conscientious or Analytic

No one style has the market cornered on problem-solving perfection and each style brings a different creative focus to project, people and process problem solving and decision making.

Let's review the four primary styles and what is important to them.

The **Dominant** has a telling style. As a result, a Dominant tends to speak quickly, directly, and intensely. Along with speaking quickly, Dominants move and process information quickly. They are project, fact, and task orientated, and interested in discussing goal achievement, results, targets, or the bottom line. Dominants don't want to spend time discussing or fussing over the intricacies of goal achievement. Project orientated, Dominants just want to know if the goals are being met and if not, why not, or what has to be done to make the goals a reality.

On a personal basis, Dominants want power and control over their environment. They operate independently and value challenge and competition. Freedom to make decisions is critical to the Dominants ability to affect their well-being and self-preservation. Dominants are comfortable taking risks and need to be in control of their own destinies.

Dominants play an important role in ensuring work groups stay focused and moving forward on important goals. Because this group places a high value on time, Dominants want results on a continual basis. It is essential for them to know things are being accomplished.

When things are not moving along at a pace that suits them, or when issues become bogged down in process or detail, Dominants become cranky. When that happens, people in this group become directive, impatient, and autocratic. What the crankiness is really about is they are not getting the results they want, in the timeframe in which they want them.

In order to help a Dominant lessen his or her anxiety over the consistent achievement of results, be prepared to talk in terms of work performance and outcomes. Give a Dominant choices or options and then ask for opinions on which way to tackle potential problems. The good news is most Dominants accept bad news well. You can identify issues or dilemmas you are facing because they love challenges and, instead of becoming overwhelmed, they will become challenged over the issues that are preventing the achievement of results.

On the downside, if a Dominant demonstrates low flexibility on a consistent basis, by only focusing on results or outcomes with little regard for how their behavior or decisions affects others, their wonderful strength of being focused and achievement-oriented can become a weakness as people perceive them to be domineering, uncaring, ruthless and rude. It is important for Dominants to remember not everyone operates at the pace and intensity they do, and it sometimes takes time to explain and educate others about what is in it for them in the achievement of the Dominant's desired results.

The **Expressive** is another style. Expressives, like Dominants, speak quickly, directly, and intensely. They also move and process information quickly. A major difference between the Dominant and Expressive is that Expressives are "people people" and value relationships as they achieve their results. Expressives are risk takers, innovators, and change agents. They tend to flourish in dynamic and uncertain environments.

On a personal basis, Expressives shine in environments that are stimulating and fast paced. They welcome new challenges as the challenges create opportunity for them to demonstrate their innovation and creative expression. Expressives will lead the charge and get people excited about the potential of a new opportunity. They like risks and want to live on the edge as they chart their personal and professional success.

Expressives are important in work groups because they are creative, innovative idea generators. They tend to have a "go-big-or-stay-at-home" attitude, so when they come up with ideas, the ideas are often wild, expensive, crazy, workable, or just plain fun. When Expressives are not given opportunities to generate and present ideas and options, or are not identified as important in the workplace, they may feel undervalued, left out, or unrecognized. In these situations expressives, over time, tend to lash out or explode. Their intense reactions are usually upclose and personal. Their lashing out is their way of saying they need to be heard and acknowledged.

When an Expressive is lashing out, don't say, "Get a life, What's your problem anyway? or Lighten up". Such statements speak volumes about the Emotional SMARTS!® of the person saying them. A more effective approach is to listen, acknowledge, and ask what can be done to turn the situation around. It is important to realize that, because Expressives operate at a fast pace, when they lash out it happens very fast and then it is over. They tend not to hold grudges because they say what they have to say, when they have to say it, almost to a fault. Expressives need to remember many other people need time and space to evaluate new ideas and related decisions, and this process takes time. Expressives need to slow down, self manage their intensity and energy, and provide the opportunity to discuss not only what to do but how to do it.

A third style is that of the **Steadier or Amiable**. These people can be the glue or heart beat of an organization because they often know more about what is happening, from a people perspective within the company, than any of the other styles. They know because they care about people, are interested in what people are feeling and thinking. They ask questions and listen beautifully. Steadiers have an asking style in that they ask questions of other people, versus having a telling, directive style. They tend to move, speak, and process information more methodically and carefully. Like Expressives, they place a high value on people and relationships and are willing to take considerable time to get to know a person.

On a personal basis, Steadiers need to know that what they are doing and how they are doing it is OK! They need approval from others and place a high value on community, participation, and family, both corporate and personal. They do not like taking risks and will obtain a number of opinions prior to making a decision that might result in their actions receiving the disapproval of others.

Steadiers play a significant role in work groups because they will champion causes for the people who are affected by the decisions a group makes. They raise everyone's consciousness of decency and respect by demonstrating their concern for others.

When decisions are made that offend, inconvenience, or violate people, Steadiers work hard to find a peaceful common ground. They will spend considerable time talking to others about their opinion on the topic at hand. Steadiers ideally want 100 percent of the group buying in 100 percent of the time on 100 percent of the issues, and they will do what they can to achieve that outcome.

Steadiers have to be careful, in their quest to obtain 100 percent buy in, harmony and a sense of community, they are not perceived as wishy washy and unable to hold their ground. They need to understand that on any issue, personal or professional, if approximately 80 percent or better of the work group or family is buying in, that is probably as good as it is going to get. It is important for them to focus their time, energy, and care on the 80 percent or better that are on board and supportive, and not spend 80 percent or more of their energy on the 20 percent of the people who are not supporting the initiative.

The last group is the **Analytics.** Analytics, like Dominants, are project, process, fact, and task oriented. The difference is Analytics approach projects wanting to evaluate all the options relating to the issue at hand. They are methodical and careful in their approach to analyzing the situation and assessing it in terms of process and procedures.

On a personal level, Analytics have a need to be respected. They place high value on being perceived as thorough, capable, and careful in their approach to issues. As a result of their focus on processes versus relationships, they hesitate to take risks, mainly because they want to be certain they have evaluated all relevant issues and ultimately made the right decision.

Analytics can think of questions about issues that seldom cross the minds of people with the other styles. Analytics are great at questioning, "How? Why? When? Where? Who? What? and, What If?" The other styles need to understand and recognize that effective analysis takes time.

The challenge for Analytics is to ensure their time, energy, and the resources spent analyzing are relevant and appropriate for the issue at hand. Sometimes, Analytics ask the questions because the questions are relevant to the issue at hand. There are times, however, when they ask questions because the question themselves are interesting to them. And sometimes, they ask questions just to ask questions. The caution for Analytics is to be careful they don't spend valuable time and resources analyzing the analysis of the analysis of the analysis.

Each of the above styles brings its unique strengths to the creative process of decision-making. The challenge for each style is to not overuse its strengths to the point where the strengths become weaknesses. This is where flexibility comes in. Flexibility is our ability to understand issues from a number of different perspectives. When we demonstrate flexibility, we are able to get out of our own way and consider the views and opinions of other people. We enhance our ability to gain feedback and endorsement from others. People who are able to gain endorsement from others are able to demonstrate a breadth of knowledge, skill, and competence in projects, about processes, and with people.

The lower the flexibility, the more people will focus on what they want, how they want it, when they want it, and why they want it. They will be hesitant to listen, explore, discuss, and evaluate the ideas and opinions of other people. They will only see things from their point of view and they will not be prepared to consider another person's needs, perspectives, or reactions.

For example, if Dominants illustrate their low flexibility by only focusing on results to the exclusion of people issues and concerns, they lessen their effectiveness with others by being perceived as ruthless, domineering, OR as a "psychopath in a suit". If Expressives only focus on what to do and give no thought as to how things could be done, they could be perceived as flighty, incompetent, or a "loose cannon". If Steadiers seek 100 percent agreement from everyone involved in situations as they attempt to gain consensus, they could be perceived as indecisive, unfocused, or "wishy-washy". The Analytic's challenge is to make timely decisions. If Analytics don't know when to move forward in selecting solutions, in time they could be perceived as ineffective, unproductive, or as "nitpickers".

The most effective and productive environments are those that incorporate and solicit input from flexible people with as many styles as possible. People with various styles will perceive the problem differently. As a result, they will identify different, but equally viable, resolution methods and outcomes. It is beneficial, when making decisions, to consider how people with some of the other styles might evaluate and respond to the same problem.

Emotionally Unaware things to do in the area of creativity are to:

- Not understand and utilize the strengths of the different styles of people with whom you work and live.

- Be inflexible, unappreciative, or demeaning about style differences.

- Demonstrate low flexibility by not stepping out of your own style. If you say you are who you are and that's just the way it is, you are really making a statement about your low flexibility. To be flexible, you must be able to appreciate other styles' point of view and be willing to integrate various thinking and work-processing patterns of all styles into collaborative, and creative problem-solving and decision-making process approach.

You are creatively employing your Emotional SMARTS!® **when you:**

- Surround yourself with people who have different styles from yourself. A common problem for new managers, supervisors, team leaders, or inflexible people, is to hire in their own likeness. When you surround yourself with people who are just like you, creativity is limited because problems only get addressed from one perspective.

- Are aware of the negative aspects of "group think". Group think is when a group of people get together to solve a problem and end up deferring to the person who is perceived as having the most power and influence in the group.

- Operate from a base of strength, not fear. Many people today, in their efforts to cope with the amount of change they are experiencing, have become embroiled in career fear. They are fearful to speak up in a positive way because they believe something bad might happen to them.

- Utilize impulse control and stress management techniques. If you need to, slow down in how you speak, process data or interact with others. For others, you might need to speed up in how you deal with others, particularly if you are a Steadier or Analytic style and dealing with a Dominant or Expressive. Adjusting your style in the creative process enables you to maximize your creative strengths, lessen the negative effects of your weaknesses, put yourself in the other person's shoes and mutually work to a satisfactory end result.

Remember, you cannot be creative if you are fearful. If you employ your Emotional SMARTS!® you recognize when you are operating from a base of fear and you take charge of the situation by becoming aware of how you feel about what is happening to you. You develop strategies to deal with the related stress, identify relationship-building activities that could result in an increased network of contacts, and make decisions on how you are going to improve the quality of your situation and life. You do not weaken or resign yourself to the situation because you are only seventeen years, four month, and three days away from retirement.

Decision-Making Skills

Quick Reference Style Guide

The following chart is a Quick Reference Style Guide that identifies general behaviors of each style group. The intent of this chart is to identify dominant traits of each style group.

The **"C"** identifies what people are interested in from a corporate or business perspective.

The **"P"** identifies what motivates people on a personal basis. (Don't underestimate these personal motivators. When the dust settles, people are often motivated to make decisions for personal reason versus anything else on this chart.)

The **"V"** relates to what people tend to value, in how these people run their lives and careers.

The **"B"** relates to how people behave, how they deal with time, how they communicate, and how they approach risk taking.

The **"T"** identifies how people react when they are under tension; when they become cranky. (Most people get cranky because they don't believe they are getting what they need corporately, personally, or from a values perspective.)

The last line relates to actions. The **"A"** identifies things we can do to demonstrate our leadership and interpersonal skills in working with people under tension. These steps can help lessen relationship tension so both parties can move on with the project, issue, or task at hand.

Quick Reference Style Guide

Dominant/Driver

C: Results, outcomes, bottom line targets, objectives

P: Power and control over environment

V: Accomplishment, opportunity, freedom

B: Project or task orientated,
Controls emotions,
Moves, speaks, processes information quickly,
Tells vs. asks in communication,
Willing to take risks

T: Directive, impatient, autocratic

A: Give options, choices, probabilities

Influencer/Expressive

C: Innovative, creative, dynamic people and places

P: Recognition, acknowledgement, creative license

V: Fairness, congruence, integration with others

B: People and relationship orientated,
Shows emotions,
Moves, speaks, processes information quickly,
Tells vs. asks in communication,
Willing to take risks

T: Verbal attack, intense, personal

A: Listen, acknowledge, seek ideas for the solution

Analytic/Conscientious

C: Details, charts, graphs, systems, processes

P: Respect, self-reliance, correctness,

V: Tradition, customs, formalities

B: Project or task orientated,
Controls emotions,
Moves, speaks, processes information carefully and methodically,
Asks vs. tells in communication,
Cautious when taking risks

T: Withdraws, pulls-back, ignores the situation

A: Give evidence, measurable or observable procedures, clarify details of the task at hand

Steadier/Amiable

C: Harmony, cooperation, stable environments

P: Approval, acceptance, fits with status quo

V: Community and family, connectedness, equality

B: People and relationship orientated,
Shows emotions,
Moves, speaks, processes information carefully and methodically,
Asks vs. tells in communication,
Cautious when taking risks

T: Goes along with others, hesitates to take a stand

A: Give endorsements from others, references, guarantees warranties

Flexibility: Gaining feedback and endorsement from others through one's:

Breadth of knowledge, skill, and business acumen in terms of projects, processes, and people.

Image that is appropriate to the environment you are in, dress, grooming, verbiage, body language, and presentation skills that enable you to effectively communicate ideas to a wide range of people.

Ability to give and receive feedback that is clear, concise, constructive, and nonjudgemental.

Decision-Making Skills

Selecting Solutions

Selecting solutions has to do with making decisions based upon the best information available. In order to make a good judgment and select the best solution, we need to take risks. This means that after assessing the available information, considering the opinions of others, projecting the best- and worst-case scenarios, and listening to our intuition, we make a decision.

We will never have enough information or answers to feel 100 percent confident in any decision. Therefore, we need to know when and how to move forward in the decision-making cycle. In the final analysis, we need to be able to make the best decisions we can based on the information, time and resources we have available at that time.

We also need to come to terms with the fact that we will never get 100 percent buy-in on 100 percent of the issues 100 percent of the time. There will always be some people who, for reasons of their own, will not support our solution or approach. We need to ensure that we do not fall into the trap of focusing extensive time, money, energy, resources, and talent on those people in an effort to gain their support. Instead, we need to focus on those who are on board, who are supportive, as they will want and need our insight, ideas, encouragement, and appreciation.

Emotionally Unaware things to do when selecting solutions are to:

- Not listen to yourself, ignore your intuition, and make decisions that appear logical but don't feel right.

- Make decisions that are unethical, illegal, or immoral.

- Act on impulse versus emotional and intellectual intelligence.

Emotional SMARTS!® let you select solutions based on your ability to:

- Evaluate options in a timely and pro-active manner.

- Eliminate irrelevant or inappropriate solutions quickly and without guilt.

- Not sweat the "small stuff". Fussing and fretting over things that are not relevant or important to the end result take up valuable energy, intellectual and emotional capital, and time. Learn to identify inconsequential issues and when to let go of them.

- Identify and manage the buyer's remorse you inevitably feel with major decisions or purchases.

Buyer's remorse is when you second guess yourself as to why you made the decision you did. You wonder if you could have gotten the product or service faster, cheaper, or better from someone else. In such a case, you need to ask yourself this question, "Did I make the best decision I could with the time, money, energy, and information I had available?" If the answer is yes, move on. If the answer is no, identify what you need to do next time to improve your decision-making abilities.

Decision-Making Skills

Reality Testing

Reality testing is exactly that. Evaluating our problem analysis and decision-making in terms of the reality of the day.

We are not always going to come up with the best or most ideal decision. Sometimes we have to make a decision that, while we are not totally crazy about it, we can live with. It's called a "trade-off".

Reality testing has to do with our ability to trade off the positives of the situation against the negatives. In this way, we can arrive at the best solution that positively maintains or improves the overall situation. If the decisions we make positively maintain or improve a situation 80 percent of the time or better, we are probably making good choices. If the decisions we make only address 20 percent of the overall situation and do not positively maintain or improve the situation, we are probably not making good decisions.

Emotionally Unaware things to do would be to:

- Make the decision anyway – when it only affects 20 percent of the issue.

- Try to ignore an important situation until it goes away. It won't!

- Look at only the short-term outcomes versus the long-term effects of the decision about to be made.

- Focus on the symptoms of a situation rather than spending the time and energy to address the core issues.

Emotional SMARTS!® means we are able to:

- Apply the SMART formula:

   S Is what I am doing **Specific**? (Do I know exactly what to do?)

   M Is it **Measurable**? (Can I measure my success?)

   A Is it **Attainable, Achievable**? (Can I really make it happen?)

   R Is it **Results-Oriented**? (Can I achieve a clear-cut outcome on this issue?)

   T Is it **Timely**? (Is it the right thing to do right now?)

Overall, the quality of the decisions you make in life goes back to how aware you are about how you feel, what you think, what you believe in, and what you hope for.

The cornerstones and characteristics of Emotional SMARTS!® are interdependent and dynamic. When you demonstrate your Emotional SMARTS!®, you are consistent, vigilant, and determined to protect your emotional wellness. You know that when you look after yourself, you are better able to care for the important people in your life and make meaningful contributions to your relationships, workplace, and community.

In Closing, for now . . .

This book about Emotional Smarts!® has discussed redefining our personal and professional competence. In the "old" days, it was enough to be technically proficient at your work. In today's workplace, you still need to be technically proficient but you must also demonstrate high self-awareness, behavior, contact and decision-making skills.

In the workplace, as in life, people want to do business and associate with people they like or respect, trust, and believe are capable of doing the job – the job of being an employee, a leader, a manager, a supervisor, a partner, a sibling, or a friend. You have a better chance of being that kind of person when you demonstrate your Emotional SMARTS!® As a result, your reputation, opportunity, sphere of influence, network of contacts, access to information, and overall accomplishments and results increase.

So now, where do you go from here? How can you make this material relevant to your emotional wellness and quality of life? A place to start is to identify the cornerstones or characteristics in which you excel. Acknowledge your pride and performance in doing a good job in those areas. Say to yourself, right now, "I am proud of myself for doing . . . achieving . . . demonstrating . . . practicing . . . having . . . "

Next, identify the area that you feel gets you into the most emotional difficulty or is the hardest for you to manage. You must understand and be able to acknowledge your feelings and thoughts about this issue before you can move forward on addressing it. Ask yourself: "What makes it hard?" Is it hard because you don't have the knowledge or skill to address the situation? Is it hard because you don't have the energy to address the situation? Is it hard because addressing the situation would mean you have to move out of your comfort zone? What is making you want to address the situation? Even more important, what is holding you back from addressing the situation? Very simply, in the final analysis you will do things for your own reasons, not for other people's reasons. You need to see value in making the desired changes or you won't make them.

I hope you see value in shoring up Emotional SMARTS!® cornerstones and characteristics in your life because I believe you will win even more than you already are, when you approach life in this grounded, centered, and focused manner. Next, when it comes to behavior, you can behave appropriately by operating in an emotionally independent manner, and managing your stresses, impulses, and conflict-management approaches. Third, your contact skills enable you to connect with others and build long-term, durable, mutually satisfying, and empathic relationships. Last, your decision-making skills will improve, as your awareness, behavioral, and contact skills improve. They will facilitate you in making smart decisions that result in attaining what is important to you. It's an evolutionary, interdependent, and positive process designed to enhance your quality of life, relationships, and results.

Bibliography

Bar-On, R. *The Era of "EQ", Defining and Assessing Emotional Intelligence.* Paper presented at the 104th Annual Convention of the American Psychological Association in Toronto, Ont., August, 1996.

Bardwick, J. *Danger in the Comfort Zone.* New York, NY: Amacom, 1991.

Beattie, M. *Co-dependent No More.* New York, NY: Harper and Row, 1987.

Beattie, M. *Beyond Co-dependency and Getting Better All the Time.* New York, NY: Harper and Row, 1989.

Branden, N. *Six Pillars of Self-esteem.* New York, NY: Bantam Books., 1994.

Cooper, R.K. and Sawaf, Ayman, *Executive EQ, Emotional intelligence in Leadership and Organizations.* New York, NY: Penguin Putnam Inc. 1997.

Danson, M. *Smart Moves for the Smart Kid in All of Us.* West Palm Beach, Fl: SmartMoves, Inc., 1996.

Farnham, A. "Are You Smart Enough to Keep Your Job?" *Fortune,* 1996, 34-48.

Foot, D. *Boom, Bust and Echo.* Toronto, Canada: Macfarlane, Walter and Ross, 1996.

Gardner, H. *Frames of mind: The Theory of Multiple Intelligences.* New York, NY: Basic Books Inc., 1983.

Gardner, H. *Multiple Intelligences; The Theory in Practice.* New York, NY: Harper Collins Publishers, 1993.

Gilligan, D. C. *In a Different Voice.* Cambridge, MA: Harvard University Press, 1993.

Goleman, D. "The Decline of the Nice-Guy Quotient." *The New York Times*, September 24, 1995a, p. E6.

Goleman, D. *Emotional Intelligence.* New York, NY: Bantam Books, 1995.

Goleman, D. *Working with Emotional Intelligence.* Canada, Random House, 2000.

Gordon, T. *Leadership Effectiveness Training.* New York, NY: Wyden Books, 1980.

Hall, F. S. "Dysfunctional managers: The next human resource challenge." *Organizational Dynamics*, 1992, 48-57.

Harris, T. A. *I'm OK, You're OK.* New York, NY: Hearst Corporation, 1973.

Inscape Publishing, *Personal Profile System.* Minneapolis, Minnesota: Inscape Publishing, 1994.

Keating, D. P. "A Search for Social Intelligence." *Journal of Educational Psychology*, Vol. 70, No 2, 1978, 218-223.

Korhaber, M., Krechevsky, M., & Gardner, H. "Engaging Intelligence." *Educational Psychologist*, Vol. 25, Nos 3 & 4, 1990, 177-199.

Knight, C. "EQ-I Aims to Measure Emotional Smarts." *Canadian HR Reporter*, September, 1996, 6-7.

LeDoux, J. E. "Emotion, Memory and the Brain." *Scientific American*, 1994, 50-50.

Leider, R. J., & Shapiro, D. A. *Repacking Your Bags.* San Francisco, CA: Berrett-Koehler Publishers, Inc., 1995.

Mayer, J. D., DiPaolo, M., & Salovey, P. "Perceiving Affective Content in Ambiguous Visual Stimuli: A Component of Emotional Intelligence." *Journal of Personality Assessment*, Vol. 54, March/April, 1990, 772-781.

Mehrabian, A. *Silent Messages.* Belmont, CA: Wadsworth Publishing, 1981.

Mayer J. D., & Salovey, P. "The Intelligence of Emotional Intelligence." *Intelligence,* Vol. 17, 1993, 433-442.

Merrill D., & Reid R. A. *Personal styles and Effective Performance.* Radnor, Penn: Chilton Book Company, 1981.

Morin, W. J. *Silent sabotage: Rescuing our Careers, our Companies, and our Lives from the Creeping Paralysis of Anger and Bitterness.* New York, NY: AMACOM, 1995.

Multi-Health Systems. *EQ-Inventory™ (EQ-i™)* [Brochure]. Toronto, Ont, 1996.

Ontario Women's Directorate *Words that Count Women In.* [Report]. Toronto, Ont, 1993.

Ormiston, S. *Brain Sex: [Review of the video program.]* Oakville, Ont., Magic Lantern Communications Ltd., 1996.

Peters, T. *Crazy Times Call for Crazy Organizations.* New York, NY: Random House. 1994.

Quinn, J. B. *Intelligent Enterprise.* New York, NY: The Free Press, 1992.

Salovey, P., & Mayer, J. D. "Emotional Intelligence." *Imagination, Cognition and Personality*, Vol. 9, No. 3, 1990, 185-211.

Schaef, A. W., & Fassel, D. *The Addictive Organization.* New York, NY: Harper Collins, 1988.

Sheehy, G. *New Passages.* Toronto, Ont: Random House, 1995.

Sternberg, R. J. *Successful Intelligence.* New York, NY: Simon and Schuster, 1996.

Stone, K.F. & Dillehunt, H.Q. *The Subject is Me.* Santa Monica, CA: Goodyear Publishing, 1978.

Stossel, J. "Boys and Girls are Different" [Review of the video program *Men, Women and the Sex Difference.*]. MPI Home Video Presentations, ABC News, New York, NY, 1995.

Tanenbaum, J. *Male and Female Realities: Understanding the Opposite Sex.* Costa Mesa, CA: Robert Erdmann Publishing, 1991.

Tannen, D. *That's Not What I Meant!* New York, NY: Ballantine Books, 1986.

Tannen, D. *You Just Don't Understand*. New York, NY: William Morrow and Company, 1990.

Tannen, D. *Talking 9 to 5*. New York, NY: William Morrow and Company, 1994.

Thorndike, R. L., & Stein S. "An Evaluation of the Attempts to Measure Social Intelligence." *The Psychological Bulletin*, Vol. 34, May, 1937, 275-285.

Weston, D. C., & Weston, M. S. *Playwise: 365 Fun-Filled Activities for Building Character, Conscience and Emotional Intelligence in Children*. New York, NY: Putnam Publishing, Inc, 1996.

Woodward, H., & Buchholz, S. *Aftershock, Helping People Through Corporate Change*. Toronto, Ont: John Wiley & Sons, Inc., 1987.

Wyatt Company *Best Practices in Corporate Restructuring: Wyatt 1993 Survey of Corporate Restructuring in Canada*. [Report]. Toronto, Canada: Author., 1993.

Walters, B., & Goleman, D. *Emotional Intelligence: An Interview on Emotional Intelligence* [Review of the interview 20/20]. ABC News, New York, NY, 1996.

The Emotional SMARTS!® Series

Business consulting, conference presentations, keynote speeches, workshops and seminars are available on the following topics:

Emotional SMARTS!® Redefining Personal and Professional Competence

Emotional SMARTS!® and Managing the Human Side of Change

Emotional SMARTS!® and Leadership

Emotional SMARTS!® and Team Building

Emotional SMARTS!® and Achieving Sales and Service Results

Emotional SMARTS!® and Effective Negotiating

Emotional SMARTS!® and Conflict Management

For further information on the series, or to learn more about the Emotional SMARTS!® self-scoring profiles and learning tools, or to book Dr. June Donaldson for your next conference, management retreat, or learning event, please contact:

Dr. June Donaldson
Donaldson & Associates Inc.
499 – 1919B – 4th Street, S.W.
Calgary, Alberta, Canada T2S 1W4
Telephone: 403-287-2244
FAX: 403-287-1212
E-Mail: jad@emotionalsmarts.com
Website: www.emotionalsmarts.com

How do I order?
Emotional SMARTS!®, Redefining Personal and Professional Competence.

Complete the form and fax or e-mail the order form, telephone, or mail a copy of this order form along with your payment selection to the address below.

Please send _____ books x $14.95 = $ _____

Shipping and handling costs (total order)_____ = $ __4.00__

  (Special rates for conference and/or large orders)

Subtotal _____ = $ _____

In Canada add 7% GST _____ (Subtotal x .07) = $ _____

Total enclosed_____ = $ _____

U.S. and international orders payable in U.S. funds/Prices subject to change without notice.

Name: _____

Title: _____

Organization Name: _____

Address: _____

Suite #: _____ City: _____ Prov/State: _____

Postal Code/Zip: _____ Telephone: (__)_____

FAX: (__) _____

  Volume pricing (over 100) is available. VISA accepted. Please allow three weeks for delivery, unless specific shipping arrangements are requested.

Identify your preferred payment method with an "X".

  Cheque   _____   Payable to Donaldson & Associates Inc.

  Money Order _____

  Purchase Order _____   Purchase Order Number_____ Date_____

  VISA   _____

Account Number _____ Expiry Date _____

Signature_____ Printed Name_____

Donaldson & Associates Inc.
499 – 1919B – 4th Street S.W.
Calgary, Alberta, Canada T2S 1W4
Telephone: (403) 287-2244
FAX: (403) 287-1212
E-Mail: jad@emotionalsmarts.com
Website: www.emotionalsmarts.com

Thank you for your interest in *Emotional SMARTS!*®

Additional Products and Services

This book is only one of a number of Emotional SMARTS!® products and services. Two Emotional SMARTS!® Self-Scoring Profiles exist for those people who wish to easily and confidentially assess their Emotional SMARTS!® competencies and skills according to the Emotional SMARTS!® model.

The first Emotional SMARTS!® Self-Scoring Profile, Form A, is a short form. It enables people to assess their abilities with regard to the four Emotional SMARTS!® cornerstones that relate to the skills of: Awareness, Behavioral, Contact, and Decision-Making.

The second Emotional SMARTS!® Self-Scoring Profile, Form B, is a longer form. It enables people to assess their abilities with regard to the four cornerstones and the sixteen different characteristics that support each of the four cornerstones.

A support tool for the above profiles is an Emotional SMARTS!® Self-Scoring Profile Facilitator Guide. It is designed for Human Resource professionals, business leaders, consultants, coaches, training and development personnel, and others who wish to use the above profiles in their work or with their teams.

In terms of Emotional SMARTS!® conference presentations, keynote speeches, and workshops, Dr. Donaldson has conducted a wide range of Emotional SMARTS!® presentations to diverse audiences. In addition, she integrates this concept with how people manage change, lead, work in teams, provide service and sales, negotiate, and manage conflict. Dr. Donaldson tailors the emotional intelligence presentations depending on the needs, uniqueness, and timelines required by the client. Men and women from a wide range of organizations and professions provide excellent reviews. Sessions range from forty-five minutes through to two days.

For organizations who wish to leader-train their internal staff to facilitate the Emotional SMARTS!® works, this service is available through Dr. Donaldson's Licensing and Leader Training opportunities.

For more information, please call:

Dr. June Donaldson
Donaldson & Associates Inc.
499 – 1919B – 4th Street, S.W.
Calgary, Alberta, Canada T2S 1W4
Telephone: 403-287-2244
FAX: 403-287-1212
E-Mail: jad@emotionalsmarts.com
Website: www.emotionalsmarts.com